UNDERSTANDING
CHICANO LITERATURE

Understanding Contemporary American Literature

Matthew J. Bruccoli, *Editor*

UNDERSTANDING
Chicano
LITERATURE

CARL R. SHIRLEY

and

PAULA W. SHIRLEY

UNIVERSITY OF SOUTH CAROLINA PRESS

Copyright © University of South Carolina 1988

Published in Columbia, South Carolina, by the
University of South Carolina Press

LIBRARY OF CONGRESS
Library of Congress Cataloging-in-Publication Data

Shirley, Carl R., 1943–
     Understanding Chicano literature / Carl R. Shirley and Paula W.
Shirley.
     p. cm. — (Understanding contemporary American literature)
     Bibliography: p.
     Includes index.
     ISBN 0-87249-575-2. ISBN 0-87249-576-0 (pbk.)
     1. American literature—Mexican American authors—History and
criticism. 2. American literature—20th century—History and
criticism. 3. Mexican Americans—Intellectual life—20th
century. 4. Mexican Americans in literature. I. Shirley, Paula W.
II. Title. III. Series.
PS153.M4S55 1988
810'.9'86872073—dc19   88–15084
                                                              CIP

For Néstor,
whom we loved

CONTENTS

EDITOR'S PREFACE

Understanding Contemporary American Literature has been planned as a series of guides or companions for students as well as good nonacademic readers. The editor and publisher perceive a need for these volumes because much of the influential contemporary literature makes special demands. Uninitiated readers encounter difficulty in approaching works that depart from the traditional forms and techniques of prose and poetry. Literature relies on conventions, but the conventions keep evolving; new writers form their own conventions—which in time may become familiar. Put simply, *UCAL* provides instruction in how to read certain contemporary writers—identifying and explicating their material, themes, use of language, point of view, structures, symbolism, and responses to experience.

The word *understanding* in the series title was deliberately chosen. Many willing readers lack an adequate understanding of how contemporary literature works; that is, what the author is attempting to express and the means by which it is conveyed. Although the criticism and analysis in the series have been aimed at a level of general accessibility, these introductory volumes are meant to be applied in conjunction with the works they cover. Thus they do not provide a substitute for the works and authors they introduce, but rather prepare the reader for more profitable literary experiences.

M. J. B.

PREFACE

Understanding Chicano Literature is a survey. We do not attempt in depth critical literary analysis, nor do we intend to write for an audience already familiar with the works discussed. We cannot discuss the writings of all Chicano authors, for to do so would be impossible. We have selected some of those whom we consider the best and most representative in all genres. This book is a primer, principally for Anglo students embarking on the study of a growing body of fine writing that constitutes quite a few threads in the intricate tapestry of American literature.

ACKNOWLEDGMENTS

Grateful acknowledgment is made to the following poets for permission to reprint parts of their work:

Alurista, *Floricanto en Aztlán*, © Copyright 1971 by the Regents of the University of California. Reprinted by permission of the author.

Abelardo Delgado, *Chicano: 25 Pieces of a Chicano Mind*, © Copyright 1972 by Barrio Publications and *Here Lies Lalo: 25 Deaths of Abelardo*, © Copyright 1977 by Barrio Publications. Reprinted by permission of the author.

Sergio Elizondo, *Perros y antiperros*, © Copyright 1972 by Sergio Elizondo. Reprinted by permission of the author.

Alma Villanueva, *Mother, May I?* © Copyright 1978 by Alma Villanueva. Reprinted by permission of the author.

Tino Villanueva, *Hay Otra Voz Poems*, 3a edición, Editorial Mensaje, 1979. © Copyright 1979 by Tino Villanueva. Reprinted by permission of the author.

We also wish to thank the following publishers for allowing us to reprint copyrighted material:

The Elements of San Joaquín by Gary Soto by permission

xiii

ACKNOWLEDGMENTS

of the University of Pittsburgh Press. © Copyright 1977 by Gary Soto.

The Tale of Sunlight by Gary Soto by permission of the University of Pittsburgh Press. © Copyright 1978 by Gary Soto.

Where Sparrows Work Hard by Gary Soto by permission of the University of Pittsburgh Press. © Copyright 1981 by Gary Soto.

Black Hair by Gary Soto by permission of the University of Pittsburgh Press. © Copyright 1985 by Gary Soto.

Emplumada by Lorna Dee Cervantes by permission of the University of Pittsburgh Press. © Copyright 1981 by Lorna Dee Cervantes.

Agua Negra by Leo Romero by permission of Ahsahta Press at Boise State University. © Copyright 1981 by Leo Romero.

Return: Poems Collected and New by Alurista by permission of Bilingual Press/Editorial Bilingüe, Hispanic Research Center, Arizona State University. © Copyright 1982 by Alurista.

Celso by Leo Romero by permission of Arte Público Press. © Copyright 1985 by Leo Romero.

Selected Poems by Ricardo Sánchez by permission of Arte Público Press. © Copyright 1985 by Ricardo Sánchez.

ACKNOWLEDGMENTS

Spik in glyph? by Alurista by permission of Arte Público Press. © Copyright 1981 by Alurista.

Extensive citations from *Chicano Literature: A Reference Guide*, Julio A. Martínez and Francisco A. Lomelí, Eds. (Greenwood Press, Westport CT, 1985). © Copyright 1985 by Julio A. Martínez and Francisco A. Lomelí. Reprinted with permission.

A NOTE ABOUT LANGUAGE

There is no single Chicano spoken language; there are several. Some Chicanos are perfectly bilingual in standard Spanish and standard English. Some speak only English, but almost all speak both languages with varying degrees of proficiency. Some are more fluent in English than in Spanish, while for others Spanish is more comfortable. Many Chicanos, especially in urban areas, speak and understand a third language, called *caló* or *pocho* or *pachuco*. This mixes English and Spanish grammars, structures, and vocabularies to form a hybrid language; it combines both languages, while adding new words and structures.

Most Chicano prose fiction is in English, but there are more and more novels and short stories published in Spanish, some with a considerable amount of *caló*. Poetry presents greater linguistic complexity; there are poems completely in English and others entirely in Spanish, but many employ both languages and even include *caló*. Frequently a poet will use all three languages in the same poem and, just as frequently, in the same line, thus reflecting a natural phenomenon in Chicano speech called code-switching. This occurs in the speech of bilingual people because a word or phrase in one language most readily occurs to a speaker at the

A NOTE ABOUT LANGUAGE

moment of utterance, not because of a lack of knowledge of the other language. Theater is much like poetry
in that it is frequently a mixture of English and Spanish,
uses *caló*, and contains much code-switching.

In this survey the original language of the titles of
all works is used, but Spanish titles have been translated into English. There are translations of all quotations written in Spanish, and all references are made as
clear as possible to those who read and understand
only English. For readers wishing to learn more about
Chicano language, several books on the topic are listed
in the suggested readings at the end of this book.

UNDERSTANDING
CHICANO LITERATURE

INTRODUCTION

To that composite American identity of the future, Spanish character will supply some of the most needed parts. No stock shows a grander historic retrospect—grander in religiousness and loyalty, or for patriotism, courage, decorum, gravity and honor. . . .

As to the Spanish stock of our Southwest, it is certain to me that we do not begin to appreciate the splendor and sterling value of its race element. Who knows but that element, dipping, like the course of some subterranean river, invisibly for a hundred or two years, is now to emerge in broadest flow and permanent action.

Walt Whitman, 1883

Whitman was inaccurate and was speaking as a Romantic when he used a popular term of his time, "Spanish," in referring to Mexicans or Mexican-Americans in the Southwest; but he was dead on the mark in his observation that the "splendor and sterling value" of the Chicano element would "emerge in broadest flow and permanent action." Indeed, Chicanos, or Mexican-Americans as they are also called, have made their presence felt in the last few decades in many areas of modern American life, including music, art, politics, motion pictures and television, education, labor, and, the impetus for this book, literature—prose, poetry and drama.[1]

This volume introduces the general reader to the fascinating creative writing of a cultural entity within the United States that is native yet seems foreign to those who have grown up in regions where few Chica-

3

nos live. Broadly speaking, Chicano literature can claim to be as old as the Spanish presence in the New World or, perhaps more accurately, as old as its presence within the current boundaries of this country. Some critics use as a guidepost 1848, the year of a treaty between Mexico and the United States through which a huge portion of land once under the dominion of the former was acquired by the latter. Most critical attention, however, is focused on the contemporary period, from approximately 1960 to the present. Chicano writing, as a so-called "minority" literature, has a long history, but until recently has been overlooked by non-Chicano "majority" readers and critics.

Chicanos are people residing in the United States who trace their ancestry to Mexico. Some families have lived within the present borders of the United States since the early seventeenth century, while others are newly arrived, either immigrants or the children of immigrants. Population estimates differ greatly and are complicated by large numbers of illegal Mexican aliens, but most sources agree on a minimum of some fourteen million. The majority live in the southwestern states of Texas, Arizona, New Mexico, California, Nevada, Utah, and Colorado, but there are many residing in other places, notably the Midwest.

They all share, to a greater or lesser degree, the Spanish language, a unique culture, a complex history, religion, traditions, and values that make them markedly different from the dominant Anglo society of this country. The two-thousand-mile-long border between

INTRODUCTION

Mexico and the United States has not been a barrier to cultural reenforcement. On the contrary, a steady flow of people north and south has served to emphasize the southwestern Hispanic heritage; thus, most Chicanos have never been fully "Americanized" in quite the same way as most other ethnic groups. Rather, they are an adaptive and creative people who over the years have assimilated elements from three cultures (Spanish, Indian, and Anglo) to form a separate, very distinct one.

There are several theories concerning the origin of the term *Chicano*; the most prominent is that it is derived from *mexicano*, which comes from *mexica* (pronounced "meshica"). Whatever its origin, the term was in widespread use by the 1950s and gained in popularity during the 1960s. Richard A. García, in his collection *The Chicanos in America, 1540–1974*, provides the following informative summary:

The word *Chicano* has always been used by Mexicans in Mexico. It is not new. But today it is used with different connotations. Although in the past it was applied to lower class Mexicans by the upper class, it now signifies a complete person who has an identity, regardless of class. In the past a Mexican-American was not considered an American; he was hyphenated—Mexican-American. He was looked down upon by Anglos. If the Chicano goes to Mexico he is considered *Pocho*, a person who is not quite Mexican. He is too *agringado* (Anglicized). So, the term Chicano has been chosen by the Mexican-American youth to identify themselves. The Chicano is basically any person of Mexican ancestry who calls himself a Chicano. It provides a sense of identification not given to them by the majority of people in the United States. This word not only furnishes an identity; it carries a whole philosophical meaning. A Chicano is proud of his heritage, a person who is responsible and committed to helping others of his people. The Chicano is a person who may be working class, or middle class; he may aspire to have material things or reject them, but he is a Chicano because he is not ashamed of his heritage nor does he aspire to be what he is not and can never be—an Anglo. Once the word is accepted, the person who accepts it philosophically accepts his heritage, his brown skin, without shame or reservations.[2]

Perhaps the earliest appearance of the term in a literary work came in 1947 in a short story, "El Hoyo" (The Hole), by Arizona writer Mario Suárez. He describes the people of a Tucson neighborhood from which the name of the tale is derived:

Its inhabitants are Chicanos who raise hell on Saturday night, listen to Padre Estanislao on Sunday morning, and then raise more hell on Sunday night. While the term *Chicano* is a short way of saying *Mexicano*, it is the long way of referring to everybody. Pablo Gutiérrez married the Chinese grocer's daughter and acquired a store; his sons are Chicanos. So are the sons of Killer Jones who threw a fight in Harlem and fled to El Hoyo to marry Cristina Méndez. And so are all of them—the assortment of harlequins, bandits, oppressors, oppressed, gentlemen and bums who came from Old Mexico to work for the Southern Pacific, pick cotton, clerk, labor, sing and go on relief.[3]

Some people today resent being called Chicano, viewing the term as pejorative, or linked too closely with a political and social movement with which they do not identify. However, it has gained in use and popularity over the last two decades to the point that for many it is a symbol of pride. It is a common term used by most Chicanos when they refer to themselves as a group, and it is the term most frequently used to designate their history, culture, and literature. Most authors and scholars and virtually all reference works employ the word. In this book, the terms *Chicano* and *Mexican-American* are used synonymously, mainly for variety of expression.

Deciding what Chicano literature is or is not can be a difficult task, with varying critical opinions to consider. The broadest and best definition is by Julio A. Martínez and Francisco A. Lomelí, who contend that it is "the literature written since 1848 by Americans of Mexican descent or by Mexicans in the United States who write about the Mexican-American experience."[4] Luis Leal, an eminent scholar of Chicano literature, believes that it "had its origin when the Southwest was settled by the inhabitants of Mexico during colonial times and continues uninterrupted to the present."[5] Leal divides Chicano literature into five historical periods: 1) Hispanic (to 1821), 2) Mexican (1821–1848), 3) Transition

(1848–1910), 4) Interaction (1910–1942), and 5) Chicano (1943–present). For information concerning events in Chicano history which provide the basis for much of the literature, the student is advised to consult the works listed under "A Suggested Reading List." While the focus of this book is on the last period, significant developments in earlier times will be discussed briefly in order for the reader to appreciate the background, the depth, and the vitality of Chicano literary expression over almost four hundred years.

The literary heritage of the Chicano people derives from three cultural and historical times: 1) the Mexican Indian period, principally prior to the year 1519, which marks the arrival of the Spanish; 2) the Spanish and Mexican period, from 1519 to 1848, the year in which the United States gained control of the Southwest; 3) the Anglo period, from 1848 to the present. These periods provide both an oral and a written wealth of myth, fable, legend, history, prose, poetry, and theater from which the contemporary Chicano writer often draws inspiration. Historically the authors have employed themes and subjects common to authors from all countries. In the modern age, however, there are several characteristic themes and subjects expressed by Chicanos writing in all genres. Among these are the themes of social protest and exploitation, the migratory experience, self-exploration or definition (which includes the exploration of myths and legends), and life in the *barrio*, the Chicano district of a city or town. There is also *La*

INTRODUCTION

Raza, the Race, which has a spiritual connotation that joins all Spanish-speaking peoples of the Americas.

Beginning in the mid-1960s, much Chicano literature became a reflection of a social and political movement, with attitudes ranging from the advocation of complete separation from the Anglo society to a stance calling for a Mexican-American cultural identification within the framework of the larger society. In the last quarter-century Chicano literature has flourished, with Chicanos writing and reading novels, short stories, and poetry more than ever before. There has been a corresponding growth in the performance of theatrical works. A great need for publishing outlets for writers has begun to be filled; among the outstanding firms are Tonatiuh-Quinto Sol in California, Bilingual Press in Arizona, and Arte Público Press in Texas. A few Establishment presses are beginning to issue works by Chicanos. Increased academic recognition has led many colleges and universities to initiate undergraduate majors as well as graduate programs in Chicano Studies, all of which include literature courses in their curricula. These developments have drawn much-deserved attention from critics, not only in traditional literary journals but also in new ones whose focus is completely or partially on Chicano literature. In addition, full-length critical literary studies are being published by major university presses.

Previously most aspects of Chicano culture were unknown to the majority of non-Chicanos; like other ethnic American literatures, that of the Chicanos was relegated to second-class status. The sheer volume of high-quality writing by Mexican-Americans is forcing the limits of American literature to expand; as the vitality and excitement of Chicano literature are being increasingly felt, it is taking its rightful place in the field of American letters.

Notes—Introduction

1. See, e.g., Thomas B. Morgan, "The Latinization of America," *Esquire* May 1983: 47–56, and Richard Rodriguez, "Mexico's Children," *The American Scholar* Spring 1986: 161–77.

2. Richard A. García, *The Chicanos in America, 1540–1974* (Dobbs Ferry, NY: Oceana Publications, 1977) vii.

3. Mario Suárez, "El Hoyo," *Arizona Quarterly* 3 (Summer 1947): 114–15.

4. Julio A. Martínez and Francisco A. Lomelí, *Chicano Literature: A Reference Guide* (Westport, CT: Greenwood Press, 1985) x.

5. Luis Leal, "Mexican American Literature: A Historical Perspective," *Modern Chicano Writers*; ed. Joseph Sommers and Tomás Ybarra-Frausto (Englewood Cliffs, NJ: Prentice-Hall, 1979) 22.

CHAPTER 1

Poetry

Chicano writers have turned to poetry more than to any other literary genre. Because of a strong oral and written tradition, as well as the physical requirements of publishing longer forms such as the novel and drama, poetic works have been relatively easy to circulate. Various journals, reviews, magazines, and newspapers published by Chicanos have given space to poetry and the short story that has usually been unavailable to longer literary works. Conditions have, therefore, encouraged the production of poetry as a social and artistic expression.

Like other genres Chicano poetry has roots that are deep and tap many sources. Its origins can be traced to pre-Hispanic texts, to writings of the Spanish Colonial period, and later to the Mexican National period. During these periods poetry was written in the Spanish language and formally depended on traditional Spanish structures. After the 1848 Treaty of Guadalupe Hidalgo, Spanish-language newspapers of the Southwest published poetry by the "new" citizens of the United

UNDERSTANDING CHICANO LITERATURE

States. These publications provided an important outlet for the Mexican-American people, and still speak today to their lives; the same social problems are expressed in contemporary Chicano poetry. Oftentimes these writers wrote anonymously but fervently on topical subjects, such as a local election.

The *corrido*, folk ballad, is an important poetic form that developed in the nineteenth century. From the verb *correr*, meaning to run, the *corrido* grew out of a rich oral tradition dating to pre-Columbian times. It served to inform and educate people about heroic deeds, catastrophes, wars, and everyday events, while at the same time entertaining them. Usually sung to the accompaniment of a guitar, *corridos* bound the Mexican-Americans together through common values and experiences; they were also another tie to Mexico, since most *corridos* were Mexican in origin. Some *corridos* originating among the Mexican-Americans dealt with subjects ranging from the death of Billy the Kid to Chicano participation in the Civil War. The best-known *corrido* comes from Texas's Lower Rio Grande Valley. Dating from 1901, the *corrido* of Gregorio Cortez relates the story of Cortez's flight from Anglo injustice after he shot and killed an Anglo sheriff.[1] This ballad, still heard in many Chicano communities, was made into a motion picture in 1982 and starred Edward James Olmos as Gregorio Cortez.

During the last half of the nineteenth century more poems by Mexican-Americans began to be written in English, and by the turn of the century it had become rather common for poets to write either entirely or pre-dominantly in English. An examination of the many newspapers that printed poetry by Mexican-Americans for over one hundred years attests to the continuity of this popular form of expression. This poetry demonstrates that a strong belletristic tradition existed within the pages of Mexican-American publications for over a century, side by side with the oral, folkloric material.[2]

The poets of the early twentieth century most often mentioned in histories of Chicano literature are Vicente Bernal, author of *Las Primicias* (The First Fruits—1910); Roberto Félix Salazar, who wrote many love lyrics during the 1930s; and the prolific Felipe Maximiliano Chacón. Fray Angélico Chávez, a Franciscan priest from New Mexico, is the best of the group and the one most often read. Fray Chávez's principal poetic contributions have been in poems to Christ and the Virgin: *Clothed with the Sun* (1939), *Eleven Lady-Lyrics and Other Poems* (1945), and *Selected Poems with an Apologia* (1969).

Beginning in the 1960s there was a burgeoning literary movement that was inseparable from the Chicano social and political movement of the same time. A struggle for social and economic empowerment as well as the fierce assertion of dignity and self-identity, the Chicano Movement found vocal expression through publications such as *El Malcriado* (The Brat), the official publication of the United Farmworkers Union; *Con Safos* (an idiom meaning something like "same to you"); *El Pocho Che* (Chicano Che, suggesting the Cuban revolutionary leader Che Guevara); *El Grito del Norte* (The Cry of the North); *El Gallo* (The Rooster); *Regeneración* (Regeneration); and *El Grito* (The Cry). These newspapers and magazines often carried poetry which expressed the context, aims, and passions of the Chicano struggle.

The period of the 1960s has been termed the Chicano Renaissance, for it signals the beginning of the contemporary period in Chicano literature. Works of drama, prose, and poetry most often discussed today have been written since the mid-1960s. Most of the writers are still alive and continue to add to the corpus of Chicano literature; therefore, clearly it is vital and changing. There are more poets worthy of mention or lengthy discussion than can be handled in a study with the present aims and limitations. The reading list and bibliography at the back of this volume should be helpful to those who wish to read more widely and/or deeply.

The poets discussed here are outstanding and representative, but that is not to say that they are the only ones who are. This work strives to introduce the major authors, themes, and forms of Chicano poetry, but with no intention of being comprehensive. The body of contemporary Chicano poetry is divided into two categories: poetry of the Chicano Movement and post-Movement Poetry. These divisions reflect broad developments in the genre that have taken place within the last two decades. Not surprisingly, given the ages of many Chicano poets, several fit into both categories.

POETRY

Poetry of the Chicano Movement

The phase of Chicano poetry commonly referred to as Movement poetry includes works that reflect the purposes of the social and political movement whereby Chicanos sought to declare their unique heritage, cultural pride, and linguistic richness. Poet and critic Cordelia Candelaria describes the relationship between the thematic and formal characteristics of Movement poetry in her excellent book *Chicano Poetry: A Critical Introduction*. She says that themes are explored through the presentation of polar opposites; for example, "*Raza* nationalism vs. universalism, Mexico and Aztlán [the Aztecs' mythical homeland to the north in what is believed to be the southwestern United States] vs. the United States, Equity and justice vs. racism, Tradition and communalism vs. capitalism, and Holism and pre-Americanism vs. Euro-Western worldview."[3] She goes on to say that these oppositions reject one set of values while claiming another which the Movement believes to be more humane and egalitarian. Formally, the poetry of this phase reveals four characteristics: 1) a predominance of traditional forms; 2) a frequent use of the imperative mood; 3) a declamatory style; and 4) what Candelaria calls "prosiness," that is, a style more like prose than poetry. Since the purpose of Movement poetry is so often moral and political, it is not difficult to understand why these formal features occur so often; the poet often commands his audience in an effort to incite it to political action or to greater self-awareness.

UNDERSTANDING CHICANO LITERATURE

A common starting point for discussion of Movement poetry is the year 1967, when Rodolfo "Corky" Gonzales, founder of the Denver-based Crusade for Justice, circulated a book-length epic poem that "provided the Chicano revolutionary movement with the first and most succinct formulation of the concept of Chicano nationalism and ideology."[4] *Yo Soy Joaquín / I Am Joaquín* provided a focus of attention for the Chicano Movement with its strong assertion of identity and pride. It enjoyed an unusually large circulation and was later made into a film by the Teatro Campesino. The poem reclaimed the Mexican Indian heritage of the Chicano while attacking Anglo oppression. Frequently viewed more as a sociopolitical statement than as a sophisticated literary work, *I Am Joaquín* nevertheless sets forth powerfully and in simple language the essential dichotomy of Chicano identity and the will of *La Raza* to survive. The polarities Candelaria mentions are present in abundance; for example, *gringo* vs. Chicano, Anglo neurosis vs. Chicano holism, impersonal technological society vs. personal traditional society.

The poem refers to many symbols of Mexican culture, such as Cuauhtémoc (last ruler of the Aztecs), Benito Juárez (Mexico's most famous president), and the Virgin of Guadalupe (Mexico's patron saint), as reminders of a rich heritage. The beginning neatly describes the condition of the Chicano in an oppressive society, who feels caught up in a world of confusion and is suppressed by Anglo society. Gonzales goes on to give an outline of Mexican history, an understanding of which will help the modern Chicano better to grasp

POETRY

his relation to the past and therefore to the present. A description of Chicano heroes—Joaquín Murrieta (a nineteenth-century California bandit, a Robin Hood-like figure), usually considered the "Joaquín" of the title; Elfego Baca (a New Mexico deputy sheriff in conflict with Anglos); and the Espinoza brothers (Colorado bandits somewhat like Murrieta)—presents a parallel to the leaders of the Chicano Movement who seek to reclaim their rights. Gonzales enjoins his people to act, to resist assimilation; in the final stanzas he reasserts his individual and collective identity, proclaiming the purity and strength of his race. He passionately cries out that he will endure. *I Am Joaquín*'s assertion of a collective identity and the challenge to assimilationist tendencies reflect important social and political aspects of the Chicano Movement.

Another passionate poet of the Movement, Abelardo "Lalo" Delgado was born in the state of Chihuahua, Mexico, in 1931. Delgado moved to Texas when an adolescent and settled in El Paso, where he attended school. The theme of identity so central to Chicano literature is explored in his poetry, as is the *barrio*, which has been described as "the life blood of Chicanismo."[5] Delgado is a poet whose work exhibits a wide range of concerns and sensibilities but which clings to the purposes of Chicano activism.

His first collection, published in 1969, *Chicano: 25 Pieces of a Chicano Mind*, employs a variety of themes and cultural figures in frequently prosaic verse. Two of his most anthologized poems are from this collection,

"stupid america" and "el imigrante." The first is re-
strained and avoids the declamatory style characteristic
of much of his work and that of most other Movement
poets. Three images tell of the Chicano artist, frustrated
and ignored by Anglo society—the sculptor, the poet,
and the painter. In free verse the poem speaks powerfully of the aesthetic contributions they could make to
U.S. society, but that will never be known because of
oppression. The poem begins:

> stupid america, see that chicano
> with a big knife
> in his steady hand
> he doesn't want to knife you
> he wants to sit on a bench
> and carve christ figures
> but you won't let him (32).

Likewise, the poet "will explode" because he is "without paper or pencil," and the "picasso of your western states" will die without having painted his
masterpieces.

In *Bajo el sol de Aztlán: 25 soles de Abelardo* (Under
Aztlán's Sun: 25 Suns of Abelardo, 1973) Delgado turns
away from declamatory verse to more introspective poems. The poetic voice here is that of the seer or vision-
ary whose "vision becomes a source of truth and
enlightenment from which the reader can extract his/
her own concept of Aztlán."[6] Delgado bases his collection on the images of Aztlán, the Mexican's mythical
homeland, and the sun, a symbol of Aztec religion.

POETRY

It's Cold: 52 Cold-Thought Poems of Abelardo, published in 1974, is a bilingual collection that speaks of disillusionment and frustration. The poet attacks society's indifference which produces misery. A section of the poem "To the Minority Health Providers of Tomorrow" demonstrates Delgado's characteristic style. Marked by an appeal to answer the needs of the Chicano, the poem stresses ideas over images and is prosaic in the manner of the early Movement poetry.

Abelardo Delgado has published several collections of poetry since *It's Cold*. In 1976 his *Reflexiones: 16 Reflections of Abelardo* turned again to more philosophical, introspective questions; in 1977 *Here Lies Lalo: 25 Deaths of Abelardo* speaks of emptiness, death, and his relationship to his audience. "Here lies Lalo./ He choked to death reading a poem/ to an audience which had already gone"(4). One interpretation of this work is that the death of the poet suggests "that both his audience—and by extension, the movement—and its informant (the poet) have reached a stage of dangerous quietude or possibly apathy."[7]

Under the Skirt of Lady Justice: 43 Skirts of Abelardo, published in 1978, is a collection of poems that returns to the theme of social justice. In 1979 Delgado distributed *7 Abelardos*, a loose-leaf collection of photocopied poems that do not meet the high level of some earlier work; *Unos perros con metralla: 25 perros de Abelardo* (Some Dogs with Machine Guns: 25 Dogs of Abelardo) of 1982 extends the focus of social injustice outside of the United States and calls for action against oppression no matter where it may occur. In 1970 Delgado co-authored with Ricardo Sánchez, Raymundo Pérez, and Juan Valdez one of the first anthologies of Chicano poetry, *Los Cuatro* (The Four). In 1982 he published a novel entitled *Letters to Louise.* It is highly personal, and draws one back to many of the concerns of his poetry.

Ricardo Sánchez is another poet who, like Delgado, cries out against a nation that rejects cultural and ethnic diversity. Born in the Barrio del Diablo (the Devil's Barrio) of El Paso, Texas, Sánchez, like many *barrio* youths who are discouraged by Anglo education, left school to join the army. Later he served time in prison on two occasions, experiences which intensified feelings of helplessness and frustration. But Sánchez went on to receive a PhD and has had a career in college and university teaching in addition to working as a poet.

Canto y grito mi liberación (I Sing and Shout My Liberation) was published in 1971, just two years after Sánchez was paroled for the second time. This collection reflects the style and concerns of the Chicano Movement of the late 1960s and early 1970s, with the added dimension of the *pinto* (prison) experience. Sánchez relates imprisonment to the themes of social oppression and injustice, seeing the prison as extending beyond the walls of his jail into society. "Soledad" speaks of the prisoner's loneliness and monotonous life circumscribed within the prison's walls:

soledad,
you lied!
no solitude or serenity here,

POETRY

just
tormented souls . . . no,
not souls (22).

And later in the poem "tomorrow will be like today,
why?/ there is no future,/ hope died/" (23).

In 1976 Sánchez published a 320-page book entitled
HechizoSpells (*Hechizo* is Spanish for spells). A combination of prose and poetry this volume addresses personal
topics, such as family and children, as well as subjects
related to social protest. In "Out/Parole" the poet uses
the metaphor of factory as prison and asks why the
poor should be condemned to meaningless work because of an accident of fate. But in "Three Days to Go"
the *pinto* poet concentrates on his desire to join the Chicano Movement because there is hope of change. He
effectively establishes parallel images of the gun and the
typewriter as instruments of revolution.

Ricardo Sánchez is one of the most important poets
of the Chicano Movement. His work expresses profound anger and frustration with "Amerikan" rejection
of ethnic pluralism, but also speaks positively of *carnalismo* (Chicano brotherhood), love of family and freedom. His commitment to the Chicano Movement has
been passionately intense, and his poetry demonstrates
his belief that art and politics must be one. His other
collections include *Milhuas Blues and gritos norteños* (Milwaukee Blues and Northern Yells, 1979), *Brown Bear
Honey Madness: Alaskan Cruising Poems* (1982), and *Amsterdam Cantos y poemas pistos* (Amsterdam Songs and
Drunken Poems, 1982).

UNDERSTANDING CHICANO LITERATURE

A frequent subject of Chicano Renaissance poetry is the figure of the *pachuco*, the zoot-suiter, a 1940s figure whose stylized dress and language identify him as outside of the majority society but at the same time as belonging to a group. His rebellion is an assertion of self-identity that has been treated in many works of Chicano literature (see the discussion of Luis Valdez's play *Zoot Suit* in the next chapter for a fuller explanation of the figure). One of the most famous poems about the zoot-suiter is José Montoya's "El Louie," which treats the death of Louie, a *pachuco*. The muted comic tone doesn't undermine the tragedy of loss, but rather betrays the affection of the speaker for Louie. Unable to fit into society, Louie dies alone. With references to Bogart movies, the poet maintains the notion of Louie as a theatrical gesturer to the end. Bruce-Novoa calls this work an excellent paradigm of Chicano literature because the poem rescues the dead protagonist from oblivion by preserving his memory.[8]

Another poet of the Chicano Renaissance, Tino Villanueva, published a fine collection in 1972, *Hay Otra Voz Poems* (There Is Another Voice Poems). Some of the themes of the Movement poetry already discussed are expressed in Villanueva's work of this period: the need of the Chicano people to act in order to save their identity and traditions, and the assertion of the self which is threatened by Anglo society. Villanueva also employs a strategy observed in many other writers of the Movement, that of detailing poetically the daily lives of the Mexican-Americans at the lower end of the socioeconomic scale. For example, in "Day-Long Day" he describes in moving cadences the back-breaking labor of the migrant picking cotton: "Sweat day-long dripping into open space;/ sun blocks out the sky, suffocates the only breeze" (38). The words of the boss attempt to relegate the children to the same future as their parents: "I wanna a bale a day, and the boy here/ don't hafta go to school" (38). But in the next stanza the parents defend their dream of a better life for their children: "Estudia para que no seas burro como nosotros" (Study so you won't be dumb like us). Meanwhile "Bronzed and blurry-eyed by/ the blast of degrees,/ we blend into earth's rotation" (39).

Villanueva writes of the *pachuco* in his poem "Pachuco Remembered." In this lyric he refers to the "esthetics existential" that set the *pachuco* apart and that make him a target of the police as well as a "brown anathema of high-school principals" (41). But it is his role as a precursor of the Chicano Movement that is perhaps most striking in this poem:

> ¡Ese! [Man!]
> Within your will-to-be culture,
> incisive,
> *aquzado* [sharp],
> clutching the accurate click &
> fist-warm slash of your *filero* [knife]
> (hardened equalizer gave you life,
> opened up counter-cultures U.S.A.) (40).

Villanueva's first volume of poetry contains many lyrics that are deeply personal and that treat subjects other than the Movement or Chicano culture. In 1984 he published *Shaking Off the Dark*, a collection that Julián Olivares describes as "an odyssey from the inner world of the self to the outer world of social conflicts."[9] Many of these verses describe the painful memories of migrant life, or the determination to hold on to one's identity while institutions, such as schools and even the Texas Rangers, threaten it from without.

Tino Villanueva compiled a significant Spanish-language anthology, *Chicanos: Antología histórica y literaria* (Chicanos: A Literary and Historical Anthology), which was published in Mexico in 1980. It makes many important writers of Chicano literature available to the Spanish-speaking reader.

Raúl Salinas, like Ricardo Sánchez and some other early Movement poets, spent time in prison. Writing from the *pinto* experience, he frequently uses images that describe the physical environment of the prison as well as suggest the alienation and rejection of the Chicano people who feel closed off from the full society. His most famous poem is "A Trip Through the Mind Jail," in which he re-creates in words the *barrio* where he grew up, which has been demolished. Memories of the *barrio* have provided solace in imprisonment, and now that it no longer exists except in his mind, he gives it new life through his poem. Another Salinas poem which is not as artful as "Trip" is "Los Caudillos," a bombastic piece which, like much Movement poetry, calls his people to throw off the yoke of oppression and act.

POETRY

Luis Omar Salinas's 1970 collection, *Crazy Gypsy*, exhibits some of the elements that define Movement poetry, such as anger toward an unfeeling society and the plight of the poor in a wealthy nation. In "Death in Vietnam" the poet communicates a quiet outrage by juxtaposing a description of a Chicano soldier's heralded return with the image of mothers sleeping in cardboard boxes. And the best-known poem of the collection, "Aztec Angel," which is frequently included in anthologies, tells of alienation. The title suggests the dichotomy of identification with the Aztec angel representing conflicting traditions.

Most of Salinas's other collections are usually described as surrealistic, although some critics stress his sociopolitical work. *I Go Dreaming Serenades* (1979), *Afternoon of the Unreal* (1980), *Prelude to Darkness* (1981), and *Darkness under the Trees/Walking Behind the Spanish* (1982) are developed out of highly sensual imagery. His 1987 collection, *The Sadness of Days: Selected and New Poems*, has some outstanding verses that communicate a fine imagination and rich style.

Angela de Hoyos was born in Mexico but grew up in the United States, largely in San Antonio, Texas. She has written two volumes of poetry that reflect the sociopolitical themes and tone of the Movement. *Chicano Poems: For the Barrio* and *Arise Chicano! And Other Poems* were written in the late 1960s but not published until 1975. In both collections she addresses many of the subjects other poets have treated, such as assimilation, social involvement, and the threat of losing one's cultural heritage. Her most recent collection, *Woman Woman* (1985), contains works in both Spanish and English with the principal theme of man-woman relationships and the assertion of the feminine self.

Another poet whose writings exhibit intense feeling about unjust dichotomies in U.S. society is Sergio Elizondo. Born in 1930 in the state of Sinaloa, Mexico, Elizondo came to the United States as a young man, illegally in 1950 and again, legally, in 1953. After serving in the U.S. army, he completed his formal education, earning a PhD in 1964. Elizondo has had a distinguished career as a professor, critic, and writer.

The volume of poetry for which he is most famous is *Perros y antiperros* (1972). This is a mordant criticism of Anglo society, the *perros* (dogs) of the title, and its treatment of Chicanos *(antiperros).* The tone and subject of the work place it well within Chicano Movement poetry, but, as Candelaria points out, the "combination of dialect Spanish with sophisticated literary technique" marks a step in the development of Chicano poetry away from some of the formal simplicities of early Movement works.[10] The book's success, then, is due in great part to the poet's wielding of language, in this case Spanish. (*Perros y antiperros* eschews bilingualism, a characteristic of much Chicano poetry, and comes to life through Spanish, with only an occasional word or phrase in English. It was published in a bilingual edition with a translation by Gustavo Segade.) The poetic voice is not a godly or heroic one but that of an ordinary man telling not "what I know, but what they told me/

POETRY

and, as a Chicano, I retell" (9). In other words, the voice is one of communal experience and history.

The thirty-three cantos form a tale of Anglo oppression and injustice which since 1848 has stripped the Chicano people of their land. "Land lost, flame of love/ Land destroyed; I am full of love" (5). The poetic voice describes the compassion of the original landowners who took in the hungry and gave them friendship, but then "The bitches burst/ scattering animals that spoke another tongue" (7). This metaphor of the bitches bursting suggests a brutal force that takes over the landscape, imposing a new order (another language) that further alienates the Chicano. Elizondo's chronicle of Chicano history uses the theme of land lost as a base for his poems, then fans out to present a panoply of experiences and emotions that include the returning veteran, racial identity, the farm worker's toil, death, hope, Aztlán, and the Anglo. In the final poem of the collection, "Camino de Perfección" (Way of Perfection), the sterility of the Anglo life style is served up in images of plastic, with the color white suggesting death in life: "with a plastic spoon in his mouth/ he was born in a white clinic" (71). The portrayal of the Anglo is unremittingly negative, and draws on such cultural icons as frozen food, a "Frenchy" dog, and a camper with a chemical toilet.

Libro para batos y chavalas chicanas (Book for Guys and Gals), Elizondo's second collection of poetry (1977), consists primarily of love poems, although the first part deals with the Chicano Movement. The love poetry is both spiritual and sensual. Woman is frequently described in terms of natural elements of the earth, such as fruits, the sea, and the desert. These metaphors suggest immutability and therefore constancy and comfort.

Sergio Elizondo's ideological intent in literature is clear: to assault threats to Chicano integrity. He has been able to combine politics and poetry in a seamless fashion. He is also respected for his collection of short stories, *Rosa, La Flauta* (Rosa, the Flute), and a novel, *Muerte en una Estrella* (Death in a Star).

Among other Movement poets who contributed to the body of protest poetry are Raymundo "Tigre" Pérez, Heriberto Terán, Juan Felipe Herrera, Juan Gómez Quiñones, and Nephtalí de León. Their individual styles express many common themes of the Chicano Movement, such as the Anglo's blindness vis-à-vis the Chicano, opposition to the war in Vietnam, the Mexican heritage, the *barrio*, and the bankrupt Anglo society. Since the social protest period some of these writers have published collections that demonstrate maturing poetic consciousness.

Post-Movement Poetry

By the mid-70s the voices of Chicano poetry were becoming less strident overall, and were veering away from the blatantly sociopolitical themes of the Movement in order to create poetry that was often more personal and less communal in its focus. This is not to say that the concerns of the Movement were abandoned, but their treatment in poetry became more subtle, with poetic considerations outweighing political ones. Some of the poets already discussed contributed to this shift away from the declamatory political verses of the Movement. Perhaps no poet represents better the bridge between protest poetry and the development of a Chicano poetics than Alurista.[11]

The poetry of Alurista (Alberto Baltazar Urista Heredia) represents the interests of the Chicano Movement in literature but also signals major changes in its expression. His first collection was published in 1971 during the heyday of the Movement, but his work spans almost two decades of recent Chicano literary history. While it is undeniable that much of his verse communicates decidedly sociopolitical themes, and often in the style described by Candelaria, he nevertheless was one of the first to open up Chicano poetry by defining its link to the Mestizo (of mixed racial heritage, Spanish and Indian) past and thereby change its language.

Born in Mexico City on 8 August, 1947, Alurista lived in Cuernavaca and Acapulco until his family moved to San Diego, California when he was thirteen. The Chicano Movement was still young when he became aware of the activities of César Chávez and the United Farmworkers Union. While a student at San Diego State University, Alurista helped found MECHA, the Movimiento Estudiantil Chicano de Aztlán (Chicano Student Movement of Aztlán) in 1967. The word *Aztlán* was not an empty symbol to Alurista and the other members of MECHA, but represented a belief in the right to reclaim the ancestral homeland of the Southwest and to assert the Chicano's rightful place in America. Aztlán continues to be a dominant image in Alurista's poetry.

More than any other Chicano poet Alurista has drawn upon the Amerindian heritage of the Aztec and Mayan world, not merely to dazzle with exotic metaphors, but in order to summon forth the collective memory of the Chicano in whom this heritage resides. The frequent use of names and words in Nahuatl (the language of the Aztecs and a language still spoken in Mexico) brings the reader's/listener's imagination and knowledge to bear on an often complex image. When Alurista uses the names of Quetzalcóatl (the plumed serpent, and one of the principal gods in Aztec religion), Cuauhtémoc (the last Aztec emperor), and Tláloc (the rain god), he calls on a historical, poetic, and spiritual heritage not previously used to such full advantage by other Chicano poets. In addition to penetrating the many possibilities of language and heritage inherent in the use of Nahuatl, Alurista has developed the dimension of ritual in his work, in the poem as performance. Cordelia Candelaria says that "Chicano poetics is grounded in ritual [and] *Alurista brought this element to Chicano poetry.*"[12]

His collection *Floricanto en Aztlán* (1971) was an auspicious debut for this highly individualistic poet. Drawing on all the evocations of *floricanto* (the Spanish words

flor and *canto*, "flower" and "song," are a translation of
the Aztec phrase *in xochitl in cuihuatl*, which means
"poetry and prayer" but suggests more, for the two
were bound in Aztec ritual), Alurista revolutionized
Chicano poetics. Although not the first writer to use
multilingualism, he blended Spanish, English, and *caló*
so artfully that some critics have since called this strategy "interlingualism." (Rather than a mere shifting between Spanish, English, and *caló*, interlingualism is a
use of all the phonetic, semantic, and graphemic possibilities of the languages.) Alurista also breaks with traditional pagination, identifying only the order of the
poems. The language and imagery of his early period
represent a significant development of Movement poetry. In the one hundred poems of *Floricanto* one sees
the themes of identity, liberation, and self-
determination. A look at two of the most popular and
often anthologized verses will illustrate the power, both
subtle and overt, of Alurista's message.

The first poem in the collection is "when raza?" a
goad to the Chicano people to throw off a fatalistic apathy and act.

> when raza?
> when . . .
>   yesterday's gone
> and
>   mañana
> mañana doesn't come
>   for he who waits
> no morrow

>   only for he who is now
> to whom when equals now
> he will see a morrow
> mañana La Raza
>   la gente que espera
> no verá mañana
> our tomorrow es hoy
>   ahorita
> que VIVA LA RAZA
>   mi gente
> our people to freedom
>   when?
> now, ahorita define tu mañana hoy

The speaker urges his audience to live in the present, not in a vague future that may never come. When he asserts that "tomorrow es hoy" (tomorrow is today) he rejects the tradition of waiting of many oppressed peoples who hope for change to happen without their intervention. The tone and second-person address are characteristic of Movement poetry which exhorts and tries to move its audience to action. Alurista's blending of Spanish and English very effectively conveys the need to abandon clichés of time; by subverting the meanings of "when," "now," "tomorrow," "hoy" (today), and especially by attacking the stereotype of "mañana," he makes it impossible for his listeners to reject the immediate needs of the present by putting them off. The proximity of the lines "mañana La Raza" (tomorrow the people) and "la gente que espera" (the people who wait) identifies *raza* as people who wait, but

POETRY

the next line suggests that people who wait "no verá mañana" (won't live to see tomorrow). The word *espera* is especially apt here because in Spanish it means both to wait and to hope; its use thereby evokes both meanings, which are significant to the call to act which the poem embodies. The first two words of the last line are a semantic duplication that underscores the need for the listener to grasp the poet's command: "now, ahorita define tu mañana hoy" (now, right now define your tomorrow today).

"when raza?" sets a tone of challenge and urgency for the first section of *Floricanto en Aztlán,* but there are other, often more subtle poems that illustrate the conflicts and hardships of the Chicano in the Anglo world. The twenty-fifth poem, "address," is a moving example of a Chicano confronting a deaf Anglo society. The situation presented is that of a man who speaks only Spanish being asked for information by an English-speaking person. The cold, statistical information requested by the Anglo is in English, with only single words or very short phrases employed. The Chicano response is, by contrast, in Spanish and in complete sentences. Here Alurista uses the two languages to reflect a divided society with no regard for the personhood of the Chicano, whose poetic lines are an attempt to assert his identity, one which cannot be contained in the formula of the questionnaire that asks for "address/ occupation/ age/ marital status." The interruption of "—perdone . . . / yo me llamo pedro" (excuse me, my name is Pedro) goes unrecognized by the Anglo "other," who remains in cold anonymity. At the end Pedro Ortega tries again to communicate his real identity by an appeal to tradition, "—perdone mi padre era/ el señor ortega/ (a veces don josé)" (excuse me my father was/ Mister Ortega/ [sometimes don José]), but the only response he receives is "race," a word that evokes all the prejudice of the majority society. For the reader who knows Spanish the last word of the poem will suggest its Spanish counterpart, *raza*, but with none of its connotations of brotherhood, unity, or pride.

Nationchild Plumaroja (red plume or red pen) of 1972 presents a more subdued, contemplative mood than *Floricanto*. Again there are one hundred poems and a continued use of interlingualism. Pagination is a radical element in this volume, as Arabic numerals are replaced by Mayan symbols. (In a subsequent edition Arabic numerals are employed.) The five sections have titles which provide an immediate link to the Amerindian world so often invoked in the collection: "Nopal" (cactus), "Xochitl" (Nahuatl word for flower, part of the expression *in xochitl in cuihuatl*), "Serpiente" (serpent), "Conejo" (rabbit), and "Venado" (deer). While resistance to the dominating Anglo culture is still an important theme, the poet writes also of *carnalismo* (brotherhood) among Chicanos, death, fear, and triumph.

The most pervasive theme of *Nationchild Plumaroja* is the birth of the *Raza*. This theme is often presented along with other themes, such as justice, but it remains the focus of the volume. In "because la raza is tired" the

POETRY

speaker reiterates the need to act that was previously described in "when raza?" The image of the sun, highly significant within the Amerindian world and frequently referred to by Alurista, concretely fixes general time in the present moment:

> because la raza is tired
> we cannot wait
> the moving red sun is out
> . . . tired, torn we cannot wait
> while la raza's being born (21–22).

In "a child to be born" the subject of *la raza* coming alive is directly linked to the Mexican Indian heritage, placing the event within that cosmogony:

> the semilla que plantó nuestro padre quetzalcóatl (the
>   seed that our father quetzalcóatl planted)
> ya germina (is now sprouting)
> en el vientre de nuestra (in the womb of our)
> madrecontinentetierra, amerindia (mothercontinentland,
>   amerindia)
> nationchild de su padrecarnalismo kukulcán (nationchild
>   of its fatherbrotherhood kukulcán) (33).

Kukulcán is the Mayan name for Quetzalcóatl, the plumed serpent. Alurista links the Aztec father of the race to the Mayan, thereby extending the symbol of father in a kind of *carnalismo*. In Aztec mythology, Quetzalcóatl was expected to return, that return being suggested by the birth of *La Raza*. The levels of meaning of the title of the book are revealed as the poems are read and as they illuminate each other.

Wordplay, word blending, and sometimes the placement of a poem on the page, are linguistic elements that help build meaning in *Nationchild Plumaroja*. For example, in "mi mind" the line "las tortillas de mi sol," (literally "the tortillas of my *sun*") ties the traditional tortilla to the image of the sun, a common enough image in Chicano poetry and one often used by Alurista. But the phonological similarity of sol/soul suggests even more, and in Alurista's poetry interlingualism prepares the reader to "hear" these sounds. Examples of word blending abound, such as "madrecontinentetierra" in "a child to be born." Some others are "carnalrojo" (redbrother) and "razanace" (raceisborn). The effect of this joining is to perceive separate ideas or images as one. In the world Alurista creates, this "new" language is necessary and effective.

Physical arrangement of lines on a page can seem arbitrary at times in free verse, but in a poem such as "I like to sleep" the meaning depends partly on that arrangement:

```
we find ourselves in a shell
      of corporation, military nightmares
of success, of co in
                co opt
                cut out
                  sp
                      lit
                          go
                              n
                                e (17).
```

POETRY

This distribution and splitting of words, especially of single-syllable words, concretely communicates the idea of fragmentation and alienation engendered by Anglo society.

Alurista's third collection of poetry, *Timespace Huracán* (1976), consists of sixty-four verses in a gentler, more reflective mode with a poetic persona that has found a calmness that does not exist in his previous tomes. Several pieces are about nature, with the natural world providing images through which the theme of Aztlán is again pursued, but in a less aggressive tone. The "timespace" of the title refers to a time-space continuum that reaffirms the bond between twentieth-century Chicano and ancient Mesoamerican, and *huracán* (hurricane) suggests motion and power. Time, space, and power/motion are the undergirdings of the being and action that the poet hopes to evoke and unleash among his *raza*.[13]

A'nque (1979) represents another phase in an already highly experimental poetic corpus. This collection of twenty-one poems and three short stories is even more esoteric than previous works, with the result that some critics have faulted it for being secretive and uncommunicative.[14] However, the linguistic play that Alurista exhibits here produces some engaging verses by reaching deeply into words as signs of meaning and sound. For instance, "jai-fai" must be sounded out for the meaning "hi-fi" to emerge. Colloquial Spanish is spelled out, as in "taba" (*estaba*) and "pos" (*pues*), and increased attention is paid to rhythm and sound.

UNDERSTANDING CHICANO LITERATURE

In *Spik in glyph?*, Alurista's collection published in 1981, wordplay often seems to be gratuitous rather than in the service of poetic communication, although there are some compelling poems. At times they fairly dance with rhythm, and the poetic persona is often more personal than one is accustomed to in the special voice through which Alurista speaks. There is a wide variety of linguistic registers, from highly cultivated English to Black English to various Spanish and Chicano forms. Always Alurista uses language as a revolutionary activity. An example of the poet's sound and wordplay is

    dare is moor
    to
    re'all i t.n.t.
    than thee i
    kan
    c (16).

Dawn's Eye, published in 1982, is part of a volume entitled *Return: Poems Collected and New* that contains a reissue of *Nationchild Plumaroja*. The *Dawn's Eye* collection is a departure in one significant way from earlier poems in that Alurista employs many more cultural references than the ones already familiar to his readers: Aztlán, the Anglo United States, and Mexico. This widening of the poet's view includes allusions to Spain, particularly the Basque country, Palestine, Morocco, Spanish Harlem, and the Netherlands, which Alurista visited and responds to in several lyrics. The wide-ranging linguistic repertoire extends also to Caribbean sounds, as in "Fire and Earth"—lava burn mon, lava hot! (128)—and lines from popular songs—"mama don't want u/ dadi don't need u" (111). The most striking of these is "xoo b do b do, clink clink, tom tom" (107).

The movement toward more personal lyrics is further developed in *Dawn's Eye*. The first two poems, " 'APA' " and "Baltazar," are loving recollections of the poet's father, and several poems deal with the poet's relationship with his wife. In "Tan" the poetic persona portrays the love of man and woman in relation to their children. In a more erotic tone "Penetra" develops from the eloquent "penetra mi cuerpo/ como la lluvia penetra/ mi huerto/" (penetrate my body/ as the rain penetrates/ my garden) to a playful breakdown of standard Spanish:

> prieta, apriétame
> tango, ganas de un beso
> tangéame—toma dos (takes two to tango)
> amé y amo, aun, a'nque? pené . . . ? (106)

No single translation can contain the myriad suggestions of the last lines, but some of the plays on words include "tango" sounding like "tengo" (I have) linked to "ganas de un beso" (desire for a kiss), but separated as the words are on the page, another suggestion is "tango" (the dance, suggesting the cliché "It takes two to tango") and "ganas de un beso" can mean "you gain from a kiss." The last utterance, "pené," appears to be a return to the first word and title of the poem, "penetra," but also is a pun, for "pene" in Spanish means penis.

The Netherlands poems in this collection deal with encountering racism in Holland, but on a more positive note they describe the sheer fun of experiencing a new culture for the first time. *Dawn's Eye* reveals the poet's heart and displays a broader crosscultural perspective than is in evidence in his previous collections of poetry. The often complicated wordplay which is an essential part of Alurista's art is more accessible here than in *Spik in glyph?* and this strategy, when combined with the personal mood of many of the poems, draws the reader into the world of the poems.

Alurista's contribution to Chicano literature cannot be overstated. He has taught Chicanos through his poetry to draw on the Amerindian heritage to define their being, and has utilized the poet's material, language, in revolutionary ways that have forever changed how we read Chicano poetry.

In the mid-1970s another shift took place in Chicano literature: Chicana (female Mexican-American) poetry began to appear more often in collected volumes as well as in magazines and journals, with the result that there was now a perspective in Chicano literature different from that of the male. The importance of this broadening perspective is summed up by Bruce-Novoa:

If Chicano poetry had begun with a focus on the man's responsibility to regenerate his culture, while the woman stood faithfully and lovingly and silently by, within ten years women had come to demand a vocal and active role in the creation of whatever

POETRY

Chicano culture was to be. This demand and its poetic expression profoundly changed Chicano poetry.[15]

"The creation of whatever Chicano culture was to be" expresses the profound impact of women's participation in the recovery, definition, and shaping of this culture. No longer silent, the Chicana's voice began to be heard in counterpoint to the Chicano and Anglo voices which had drowned it out before.

Bernice Zamora published a volume of poetry in 1976 entitled *Restless Serpents*, bound jointly with José Antonio Burciaga's collection of the same title. The artistry and Chicana consciousness of Zamora's work continue to resonate. *Restless Serpents* speaks through a poetic voice that is always conscious of being woman, Chicana, and poet. The title *Restless Serpents* suggests the Aztec serpent deity, Quetzalcóatl, who represents the creative poetic spirit, and the Freudian phallic symbol of Western culture that seeks to dominate the female. The tension inherent in this complex allusion is further intensified by the qualifier "restless," which suggests discomfort with both traditions. "Penitents," the first poem of the collection, draws on a ritual practiced in New Mexico for centuries by the *penitentes*, a male religious sect whose customs include a reenactment of Christ's crucifixion. The serpent imagery appears for the first time here. This poem's significance within the context of the entire volume is multiple: it evokes a ritual peculiar to the Chicano community of New Mexico; there is a male/female dichotomy inherent in the sacred rites; it combines the Aztec/Nahuatl religiopoetic tradition with the Mexican/Catholic tradition through the serpent imagery; and there is an underlying eroticism, a subject of many other poems in *Restless Serpents*. Zamora's poems are often battlegrounds wherein the female struggles against sexual roles imposed by society and her desire for a wholesome relationship with the male.

Perhaps more than any other Chicana poet Bernice Zamora employs allusions to Anglo-American literary texts and figures. This intertextual play links her to the Anglo literary establishment even while she acts as a critic of those male writers by providing a feminine voice to fill in the breach created by a single perspective. In "Sonnet, Freely Adapted" Zamora draws on one of Shakespeare's best-known poems, sonnet 116 ("Let me not to the marriage of true minds/ Admit impediments. Love is not love/ Which alters when it alteration finds"). Instead of a definition of love in the masculine sonnet tradition, the Chicana poet chides her male friend, apparently for asking why she likes the company of gay men. She asserts that masculinity is "a gentle, dovelet's wing" and rejects the macho image of the boxer. *Restless Serpents* established Bernice Zamora as a major poet. It is a work of conflict, ambiguity, irony, and power communicated through often brilliant language. Zamora bestrides Anglo and Chicano literary worlds, proclaiming through her poetry the essence of the Chicana artist.

Another prominent poet, Alma Villanueva, was born in 1944 in California and raised by her Mexican grandmother. She published two poetry collections in 1977, *Bloodroot* and *Poems*; the latter volume won the first prize for poetry in the third Chicano literary prize competition at the University of California, Irvine. Her third volume, *Mother, May I?* was published in 1978. Villanueva's work is autobiographical and focuses on her emergence as woman and poet.

Bloodroot expresses Villanueva's "nostalgic desire for a return to an original, maternal womb from which, presumably, both women and men emerged."[16] This vision of the cosmic womb is conveyed through such images as blood, milk, and breasts, as well as earthy images of trees and birds. The woman seeks to give birth without the aid of man through union with the earth, suggesting a common origin for everyone. In "ZINZ" the poet similarly affirms the oneness of human beings, male and female, in images referring to a common origin. The poet eventually speaks in a more personal vein in a poem reminiscent of Walt Whitman. "I Sing to Myself" describes the emerging self which cannot be held back: the woman gives birth to herself.

In *Poems* the personal voice is heard more strongly as it challenges male sexual and literary dominance. The speaker boldly asserts female sexual superiority and claims a magical witch nature in images and metaphors that continue to underscore the theme of the self emerging. This self, which is female *and* poet, also attacks the tradition of the woman as muse who inspires art. She goes on to assert that she will be her own muse and grow her own wings.

UNDERSTANDING CHICANO LITERATURE

Mother, May I? is an autobiographical narrative poem that traces the poet's development from childhood to her thirties in three sections. The theme of birthing treated in previous works continues to be developed here, but it is enhanced by the autobiographical shape of the volume and its narrative sequencing. This structure makes the reader a witness who is present when the little girl is reprimanded for examining her feces, which she associates with giving birth, an error presumably caused by her overhearing an adult conversation about childbirth which she mistakenly believes to be about bowel movements:

I
hear them talking sometimes:
–you have to push it out
hard.—I do that (7).

This inversion of expelling feces as a creative act suggests that the girl will have a special way of regarding birth and creativity, but more important is the repression she experiences from adults who stifle her natural urges. The poem/life that is displayed is a continual effort to break out of the bonds imposed by others.

The preservation of the self in a milieu that is often harsh and unloving is a theme that pervades many of the life events that we witness through the poet's eyes; the threat, and sometimes reality, of death is frequently present. When her beloved grandmother dies, the little girl's gesture of throwing a rose into the grave is pregnant with meaning for, as she tells us, "they didn't know the rose/ was me" (19). The metaphor of the rose returns at the end of the third section when in the poem "(me)" the speaker refers to herself as both "a bastard rose" and "a wild rose," and finally advises

> you must recognize
> a magic rose
> when
> you see it (39).

Alma Villanueva's chief poetic concern is with exploring her feminine self rather than her Chicana self, a dominant theme in Bernice Zamora and others. Villanueva plumbs the themes of birth, renewal, and survival in her own idiom. As Marta Ester Sánchez says, "The poetic enterprise of *Mother, May I?* is to create from concrete experience a personal myth of a universal womanhood."[17] Villanueva accomplishes this in part by challenging the restrictive psychic environment imposed by men and society, and sometimes even by other women. Her poetry stands up to this threat to authentic—that is, free—existence.

Another Chicana poet who has added a significant work to the body of Chicano literature is Lorna Dee Cervantes. *Emplumada* (1981) is a highly sophisticated collection of poems that manifest the concerns of the feminist poet. Subjects are wide-ranging and include domestic violence, identity, social oppression, nature, time, death, and poetry. One of Cervantes's most beautiful poems from this volume is "Beneath the Shadow of the Freeway," a narrative of three generations together forming "a woman family." The grandmother's quiet nurturing contrasts with the mother's cynicism. Their daughter/granddaughter listens to them both as the new freeway under construction gets ever closer to their home. The concluding stanzas state that the interloping freeway is now "across the street" as the girl now reflects her mother and grandmother in dress and actions. In another poem, "Freeway 280," the poetic voice describes the neighborhood apparently destroyed by the freeway, but the speaker has returned in hopes of finding part of herself that was lost with her neighborhood. The refusal of plant life to die and the return of the people to gather food suggest the indomitability of the *Raza* who persist in the face of technological blight. When this poem is read in the context of the previous one, "Beneath the Shadow of the Freeway," its meaning is enhanced by its association with the vivid picture of the women who used to live in the neighborhood.

"Poem for the Young White Man Who Asked Me How I, An Intelligent, Well-Read Person Could Believe in the War Between Races" is a rebuke of the smug notion of a casteless society. The speaker describes a violent, warlike world, then contrasts it with the wounds of oppression:

> . . . my stumbling mind, my
> "excuse me" tongue, and this
> nagging preoccupation
> with the feeling of not being good enough (36).

The tone of Cervantes's "revolutionary" poem ("I am not a revolutionary./ I don't even like political poems") is one of quiet outrage, which is quite different from that of Movement poetry, which is generally hortatory and appeals to the indigenous past.

The title poem of the collection returns the reader's attention to the various meanings of *emplumada*: "feathered, in plumage, as in after molting," suggesting change and maturity; and "pen, flourish" (*pluma* is "pen" in Spanish), referring to the poet's instrument and activity. "Emplumada," the last poem of the volume, addresses a favorite subject of Cervantes, the transitory nature of experience and the human response to it. The first stanza describes "snapdragons withered" at summer's end. The woman hates "to see/ them go" and thinks of "when the weather was good" (66). Her glimpse of two hummingbirds mating suggests the need to find meaning in one's intimate life while keeping the harsh world at a distance. The lives of humans, like those of flowers and birds, are brief. But the poem remains to give meaning to life.

Lorna Dee Cervantes displays a sophisticated refinement in her work which, paradoxically perhaps, also appears earthy. Even when she deals with subjects that have been written about many times in Chicano poetry, she infuses them with new meaning through her polished style. As one of the editors of a widely respected chapbook series, *Mango*, she has contributed to a growing body of outstanding poetry by Chicano and Chicana writers. Bruce-Novoa's appraisal of *Emplumada* as "among the best Chicano books ever published" is justly deserved.[18]

UNDERSTANDING CHICANO LITERATURE

Among other Chicana poets who have broadened the formerly male scope of themes and attitudes in Chicano literature are Lucha Corpi, Evangelina Vigil, Pat Mora, and Ana Castillo. Corpi's *Palabras de Mediodía/ Noon Words* (1980) treats male-female relationships, erotic love, and the conflict experienced by a woman participating in two cultures, the Chicano and the Mexican. *Palabras* was written entirely in Spanish, an indication of Corpi's strong identification with her Mexican background. It was published, however, in a bilingual format, with translation by Catherine Rodríguez-Nieto.

Evangelina Vigil has published a chapbook of poems *Nada y Nade* (1978), and two other collections, *Thirty an' Seen a Lot* (1982) and *The Computer Is Down* (1987). Her work is communicated through a strong, independent, feminine voice and speaks of family, the *barrio*, love, and loneliness. In *Thirty an' Seen a Lot* Vigil sometimes invokes other Chicano writers, such as José Montoya, author of the poem "El Louie," and Américo Paredes, a writer and scholar. Her work often demonstrates a wry sense of humor as it cuts through social (and sexist) clichés. Her last book of poetry, *The Computer Is Down*, is a trip through a modern city, cold yet personal, dehumanizing yet rooted in tradition.

Like some of the other works mentioned above, Ana Castillo's *Women Are Not Roses* (1984) rejects the worn-out stereotype of the delicate female whose purpose is to inspire, not act. Her poetic voice proclaims women's sexuality and freedom.

POETRY

Pat Mora's *Chants* (1984) is firmly grounded in the Texas desert. This El Paso poet writes evocatively of the power and beauty of the desert as well as the people who live in it. Mora describes their lives principally through emotions, such as anger, affection, envy, and passion. Her poems reflect a traditional life in a land that is both Mexican and American. Mora's latest collection of poetry is entitled *Borders* (1986).

Another fine poet of the last decade is Inés Tovar. Her 1977 collection *Con razón corazón* exhibits the influence of Alurista, particularly the Amerindian aspect. The poems of *Con razón corazón* explore the themes suggested by the title: love (*corazón* is "heart" in Spanish) and reality (*razón* means "reason" or "right"). But Tovar's poems often are ambiguous, and linguistically playful in Alurista's style.

One of the most celebrated contemporary Chicano poets is Gary Soto. He has received recognition from outside Chicano circles, and this is partially reflected in his many awards, among them the Academy of American Poets Prize in 1975 and the United States Award of the International Poetry Forum in 1976.

Soto's poetry differs markedly from that of the Movement poets already discussed, for it does not call its readers to action, nor is it declamatory. It also eschews the often idealized elements of home and *carnalismo* found in so much Chicano poetry. But it does reflect a Chicano consciousness of racial identity and the despair that can come from poverty and alienation.

UNDERSTANDING CHICANO LITERATURE

Many critics have discussed his skill as an artificer of language.

Gary Soto was born in 1952 in Fresno, California, which is located in the San Joaquin Valley, a fertile and productive agricultural area. This geographic background thoroughly informs his first collection of poems, *The Elements of San Joaquín* (1977). The volume's three divisions include powerful vignettes of Fresno, field work, and private visions of humans in an often meaningless landscape. Several poems deal with violence—for example, "The Underground Parking," where "A man who holds fear/ Like the lung a spot of cancer,/ Waits for your wife" (5). In "The Morning They Shot Tony López, Barber and Pusher Who Went Too Far, 1958" the death of López is described in terms of his birth, an identification of subjects that takes the poem beyond the realm of the journalistically sensational and into the poetic.

In some of the agricultural pieces the human beings are so closely identified with the physical world that at times they *are* the world. The poetic voice in "Field" is described as "becoming the valley,/ A soil that sprouts nothing/ For any of us" (15). One of the finest lyrics of the volume is "Field Poem," in which the narrative voice tells what he and his brother won't be able to do with their pay, such as go to a restaurant or a dance. The final image bitterly but economically communicates the situation of the farm workers:

From the smashed bus window,
I saw the leaves of cotton plants

POETRY

Like small hands
Waving good-bye (23).

The last poem of the collection, "Braly Street," is a reminiscence of a home long since torn down and replaced by factories and warehouses. Much of the language refers to earth, grass, weeds, and asphalt, other "elements" of San Joaquin that hold childhood and family memories. Where his house once stood is now "An oasis of chickweed/ and foxtails," and "The long caravan/ Of my uncle's footprints/ Has been paved/ with dirt." One remaining remnant of the past is the chinaberry tree:

I come to weeds . . .
To the chinaberry
Not pulled down
And to its rings
My father and uncle
Would equal, if alive (56).

José Varela-Ibarra has commented that Soto's *San Joaquín* poems are essentially rural and urban landscapes while his second collection of poetry, *The Tale of Sunlight* (1978), treats inner space.[19] Soto does explore the inner world of the emotions as well as memory here, and the mood is not as bleak as in *San Joaquín*; indeed, events are at times even magical. The poet evokes his childhood self in the first poem, "El niño," through an action that reminds one of a fairy tale: the childhood persona emerges from a spark produced from striking a rock and the past appears. The poet's alter ego, Molina, touches shovel, chinaberry, incinerator, a stone walk, bringing back the world of the child. At other times he both explores the world he lives in and creates new ones, as when he draws over a map with a pencil and selects a point near the Orinoco River as his birthplace. The last line expresses the boy's fantasy of an exotic Latin American place of origin unlike the true one that is often bleak and painful.

The second section of poems is sometimes humorous, as in "Litany" ("after a Mexican prayer of the poor"), where the icons of the saints are called on:

> Burnt match of San Lucas, guide us home.
> Suitcase of Santa Catarina, the donkey won't get up.
> There is a shoe for each foot, a cuff for each wrist,
> More plates than forks. Amen (33).

In "How an Uncle Became Gray" Soto draws on the magical quality of contemporary Latin American literature. The poem, dedicated to the Colombian author Gabriel García Márquez, reminds one of the head of the family whose history is the subject of the novel *One Hundred Years of Solitude*, as the uncle finds himself enveloped in butterflies that have followed him home:

> They gave off
> The silver dust
> A coin couldn't match,
> The silver that laddered
> His sideburns (40).

This episode is similar to a "magical" one in the Colombian novel.

POETRY

The Manuel Zaragoza poems comprise the third part of this collection. Manuel is a poor Mexican peasant who tries to think of ways to overcome his poverty, loneliness, and boredom in Taxco, Mexico. He considers such diverse schemes as peddling urine to tourists as the bath water of the holy virgin Olga or forming a circus. The title poem of the volume tells of a shaft of light that refuses to go away and destroys what it touches, including Manuel's finger, which it snaps off. The last poem, "The Space," expresses Manuel's philosophy of survival, for he claims that the small things that are free for the poor are enough: the natural elements—bird, moon, sun.

In 1980 Slow Loris Press published a chapbook of Soto's poems, *Father Is a Pillow Tied to a Broom*, a collection of fascinating pieces that generally develop the theme of the sadness of absence expressed in the first poem, "Concha." The little girl/narrator invokes childhood by thinking of the place where she lived and is once again a child. But the reader finds no sentimentality here: her mother, she thinks, is crazy, and her father is the image expressed in the title of the volume, a pillow tied to a broom which the child punches, calling him a drunk. Now this father lives only in her memory and imagination. The striking imagery of this first poem and its obdurate refusal to embrace sentimentality are characteristic of this slim collection. Several poems deal with violence to children by parents, and some with the abandoned and forgotten ones of society.

Where Sparrows Work Hard (1981) evokes the biblical

image of God's protection—"His eye is on the sparrow, and I know He watches me" (traditional hymn). The middle class contrasts sharply in many of these poems with the poor who keep them fed and clothed by their manual labor. Images of Anglo culture, particularly from television, underscore the chasm between classes here. In the poem "TV in Black and White" farm workers toil in a vineyard while Ozzie Nelson, a television star in a 1950s family comedy, lives in the neat, unattainable world of the golf course.[20] In another vein "There" describes a return to the narrator's old neighborhood home, similar to the journey back of "Braly Street" from *The Elements of San Joaquín.* The speaker finds that time and neglect have ravaged the place where clean washing used to hang on the line. Now he sees "the filth of bottles, gutted mattresses,/ A dead cat on its rack of weeds" (56).

Black Hair (1985) is a departure in mood from previous collections of Soto's poetry. The economical, acute images are still present, but the desolate feelings so often described in previous poems are usually replaced by more hopeful ones. The title poem captures the physical and emotional states of boyhood in the first line: "At eight I was brilliant with my body." But it develops these states by tying them in with the speaker's idolizing of a baseball player, Hector Moreno:

> When Hector lined balls into deep
> Center, in my mind I rounded the bases
> With him, my face flared, my hair lifting
> Beautifully, because we were coming home
> To the arms of brown people.

POETRY

The sense of belonging to a race and a community is significant here but, as is characteristic of Soto's work, not idealized. In the previous stanza the speaker reveals his need for the game and the hero:

> What could I do with 50 pounds, my shyness,
> My black torch of hair, about to go out?
> Father was dead, his face no longer
> Hanging over the table or our sleep,
> And mother was the terror of mouths
> Twisting hurt by butter knives (3).

Black Hair chronicles a life, from the boy of eight through adolescence, young manhood, and fatherhood. Humor untouched by sadness is allowed more space here. In "Heaven" the speaker describes a typical adolescent moment spent with a friend listening to rock and roll music on the radio. Their physical gyrations—"bouncing/ Hard, legs split, arms/ Open for the Lord"—don't end when one of the boys crashes through the screened window into a bush:

> His shoulders locked
> Between branches,
> His forehead scratched,
> But still singing,
> "Baby, baby, o baby" (23–24).

Several poems reveal the speaker's rediscovery of the world with his daughter. In "Where We Could Go" the father and child explore Paris, and in "Autumn with a Daughter Who's Just Catching On" they feed sparrows in the park. In "Hunger among Crabs" the speaker confesses, "I've been translated into three languages/ And

UNDERSTANDING CHICANO LITERATURE

still I don't make sense/—or so says my daughter," who is crying because he has shouted at her.

Gary Soto has added significantly to an already fine body of Chicano poetry. Bruce-Novoa refers to his work as "a new high in craft and a definite shift toward a more personal, less politically motivated poetry."[21] Soto eschews many of the clichés found in earlier Chicano poetry which sought to promote Chicano heritage and culture in favor of a deeper, personal perspective developed through beautifully wrought images.

Alberto Ríos is one of the most outstanding Chicano poets currently writing. His work is both folkloric and sophisticated, simple yet complex. Some of his poems have been included in such volumes as the *Norton Anthology of Poetry* and *Fifty Years of American Poetry, 1934–84*, and he has published poems in scores of magazines.

Whispering to Fool the Wind (1984) establishes a magical world where unusual events are the norm. The title of the collection suggests an intention to trick nature, exactly what many of the poems do. In "True Story of Pins," Uncle Humberto dies of rage because the seamstress won't give him the pins he needs in order to stick his captured butterflies to the wall. The seamstress finds out why he wants the pins from the southerly wind who told her.

One of the most fascinating poems in *Whispering* is "Nani," meaning "grandmother." It is written in the form of a sestina, a very demanding type of verse in which the six end-words of the first stanza must be used as end-words in the next stanza, but in a different order. Ríos's poem escapes the artificiality expected in the sestina, for his work has the sound of truth. It is about the language of love, which is expressed by the grandmother's feeding her grandson. Lacking a common language (she speaks Spanish, he English), the two people create a language of food through which they convey the happiness of being together.

Ríos's work tends to be narrative while still communicating in powerful images. He creates characters and stories as if he were writing prose, but his aim is to open a poetic world where image and human experience join forces. In "El Molino Rojo" (The Red Windmill) from *Sleeping on Fists* (1981) the poetic voice describes a world where the dead cannot leave because they have nowhere to go, and yet no one listens to them because they are dead. Here death does not provide the orderly ending that one has come to expect, but rather a disharmonious absence.

A 1985 collection entitled *Five Indiscretions: A Book of Poems* continues the prose-poem style of earlier works. One reviewer has called them "artful and haunting, like the realized dreams afforded us by such great meditative filmmakers as Bergman and Buñuel."[22] A hauntingly surrealist quality is often present in Ríos's work, but the poems are nonetheless true for their insights into human experience. While often technically brilliant, the poems still speak the language of his characters. Alberto Ríos has displayed considerable literary gifts with which to communicate his vision of growing up along the U.S.–Mexican border, a child of two cultures. But his poetry also reveals another border, the one between the inner self and the outer world.

Leo Romero is a New Mexican poet whose work includes the chapbook *During the Growing Season* (1978); *Agua Negra* (1981), which won the Pushcart Prize "Best of the Small Presses" competition; and *Celso* (1985). The latter two collections draw together many poems previously published in literary magazines.

New Mexico is a strong presence in Romero's poetry. *Agua Negra*, the name of a village in New Mexico where many people believe that Christ's face once appeared on an adobe wall, is an attempt to "construct a history/ where there are no written records" (39). The land depicted here is often frightening; people hear sounds outside their doors, only to find when they open them that no one is there; at times ghosts appear, and a belief in witches is ingrained in the people. The poet finds the "history of this valley" in local legends, in a beautiful but intimidating nature, and in his own family. *Agua Negra* is written in English and contains verses of beautiful simplicity: for instance, "The wind deftly weaving the rain/ into darkness/ as the trees wave" (41).

Romero's most recent collection, *Celso*, is an imaginative walk through life with a rogue who makes up stories so that his listeners will keep pouring him drinks. Celso plays on his townspeople's superstitions—as when he relates a fictitious encounter with the Virgin Mary; but he starts to believe his own fiction, that she is sad because of the villagers' sins, and he heads home "Probing his heart and soul." Celso's tales are often lyrical. In "Dancing with the Moonlight" he tells of falling in love with moonbeams:

> When moonlight gets into your brain
> it is called madness
> but when it gets into your heart
> it is called love (37).

Philosopher, town drunk, teller of tales—Celso is all these things and more. Through his character we see not only him but also a New Mexican village, a land, and a way of life. *Celso* has exerted such appeal that theater critic/director Jorge Huerta has adapted Romero's work for the stage. *I Am Celso* has been performed as a one-man show starring Ruben Sierra, who collaborated with Huerta on the adaptation.

Leo Romero's work joins the growing list of Chicano writers who have continued to redefine and shape contemporary American letters. His poetry reminds one of other currents in contemporary literature, such as the magical realism of Latin America and the mythical power of another New Mexican writer, Rudolfo Anaya. But Romero's clear poetic voice is also very special, for it conjures a personal and compelling vision of a place, his New Mexico.

There are many other writers whose works add to the vitality of Chicano poetry. Among them are Reyes Cárdenas, Carmen Tafolla, and Lin Romero; many fiction writers and scholars have published some exciting poetry, including Bruce-Novoa, Tomás Rivera, Miguel Méndez M., and Cordelia Candelaria. The abundance and high quality of Chicano poetry attest to its vitality and its importance in the verbal expression of Chicano culture. Linguistic variety continues to be a mark of Chicano poetry. Works composed completely in Spanish or English, a mixing of the two, and the use of *caló* underscore the multiple verbal possibilities inherent in this poetry and provide an element that enriches the entire body of American literature.

An impressive aspect of the writing of the last decade is the variety of themes displayed, a considerable broadening when compared with much of the poetry of the 60s and 70s. This is not to say that Chicano poetry does not still plumb the question of identity, life in the *barrio*, the migrant experience, and the indigenous past. But it has continued to find new depths of thought and feeling as well as the poetic richness with which to express them. The passions of protest poetry are still legitimate and in evidence, but Chicano poetry has also found passion and relevance in verses that propound universal themes, such as love, nature, and death.

Notes

1. For a full account of this *corrido* see Américo Paredes, *With His Pistol in His Hand: A Border Ballad and Its Hero* (Austin: University of Texas Press, 1958). This book-length study also discusses the history of and legends surrounding this ballad.

POETRY

2. See, e.g., Doris L. Meyer, "Anonymous Poetry in Spanish-Language New Mexican Newspapers: 1880–1900," *Bilingual Review/Revista Bilingüe* 2,3 (Sept.-Dec. 1975): 259–75.

3. Cordelia Candelaria, *Chicano Poetry: A Critical Introduction* (Westport, CT: Greenwood Press, 1986) 40.

4. Eliúd Martínez, "Rodolfo ('Corky') Gonzales," *Chicano Literature: A Reference Guide*, ed. Julio A. Martínez and Francisco A. Lomelí. (Westport, CT: Greenwood Press, 1985) 223.

5. Francisco A. Lomelí and Arcadio Morales, "Abelardo ('Lalo') Delgado," Martínez and Lomelí 200.

6. Lomelí and Morales 202.

7. Lomelí and Morales 203.

8. Bruce-Novoa, *Chicano Authors: Inquiry by Interview* (Austin: University of Texas Press, 1980) 115.

9. Julián Olivares, introduction, *Shaking Off the Dark* by Tino Villanueva (Houston: Arte Público Press, 1984) 8.

10. Candelaria 130.

11. For further discussion of Alurista's role in this development see Candelaria 71–108.

12. Candelaria 92.

13. Candelaria 163.

14. See, e.g., Alfonso Rodriguez, review of Alurista's *A'nque: Collected Works, 1976–79, La Palabra* 3:1–2 (Spring 1981): 146–47.

15. Bruce-Novoa, "Chicano Poetry," Martínez and Lomelí 170.

16. Marta Ester Sánchez, *Contemporary Chicana Poetry: A Critical Approach to an Emerging Literature* (Berkeley: University of California Press, 1985) 28.

17. Sánchez 28.

18. Bruce-Novoa, "Chicano Poetry," 170.

19. José Varela-Ibarra, "Gary Soto," Martínez and Lomelí 382.

20. Candelaria 210.

21. Bruce-Novoa, *Chicano Poetry: A Response to Chaos* (Austin: University of Texas Press, 1982) 210.

22. Ray Olson, review of *Five Indiscretions, Booklist* 1 May 1985: 1231.

CHAPTER 2

Theater

Most accounts of the history of Chicano theater use 1965 as a convenient year of origin, for this refers to the Delano, California, grape strike and the sociopolitical plays performed then by El Teatro Campesino (The Farm Workers Theater). This date is accurate, but only if Chicano theater is seen as strictly associated with political and social movements and the popularization of the term *Chicano.* While it cannot be denied that a large percentage of modern Chicano drama *is* political or social in nature, to link it or any other artistic manifestation of the Chicano people strictly to a contemporary movement is to ignore several centuries of tradition.

In the case of the writing and performing of dramatic works in the Spanish language in the United States, one can argue for a year as early as 1598 to signal origins. On 30 April, 1598 one Captain Farfán, a soldier in Spanish explorer Juan de Oñate's expedition, presented a play near present-day El Paso, Texas. This work, now lost, was a dramatic re-creation of the expe-

THEATER

dition party's encounter with the native Indians. Its performance and others like it provide evidence that the Spanish conquistadores brought with them the theater tradition of their "Golden Age" (ca. 1500–1650) and the works of such masters of the drama as Lope de Vega, frequently referred to as the Spanish Shakespeare. The native Maya, Aztec, and other Indians had their own ritual theater, so there was a ready audience for plays performed by the conquerors. Unfortunately only a few examples of pre-Columbian drama have survived, but one, *Rabinal Achí* (Rabinal Warrior), provides conclusive evidence that a strong native dramatic tradition existed and that the conquered peoples were a trained and ready audience for theatrical works.[1]

One of the goals of the Spanish in the New World was the conversion of the natives to the Catholic religion, and priests quickly realized the value of drama in the education process. Most of the early plays were Bible stories, adapted for an illiterate audience. As the conquerors spread out and established new missions and settlements, they took their theater with them,[2] and the works proved so popular that even today some are presented in churches in the Southwest. Examples of the most frequently performed throughout the years are *Los Pastores* (The Shepherds), a Christmas play, and *Las Cuatro Apariciones de la Virgen de Guadalupe* (The Four Appearances of the Virgin of Guadalupe), the story of Mexico's famous religious figure. Perhaps the most popular is *Los Moros y los Cristianos* (The Moors and Christians), which depicts the Spanish version of their fifteenth-century conquest of the Moorish invaders.[3] It can be seen annually in many towns today, sometimes performed in fields with the actors on horseback. It has been documented that this play was first seen in what is now the state of New Mexico on 8 September, 1598.[4] These works and others like them provide evidence that religious folk dramas were widely popular in what is now the state of New Mexico and, to a lesser degree, in all areas of the Southwest.

Amateur theater of a nonreligious nature apparently was also common, but at a later date—the nineteenth century. One surviving fragment of a play written around 1845, *Los Tejanos* (The Texans), is a forerunner of the kind of drama later produced by such groups as El Teatro Campesino.[5] *Los Tejanos* documents the Santa Fe expedition of 1841 in which a large group of Texans, fresh from their victory over Mexico in 1836, invaded Mexico (now the state of New Mexico) in an attempt to expand their newly acquired territory. It is a classic Good (Chicano) versus Bad (Anglo) dramatic confrontation so popular in the theater of the 1960s and 1970s.

Professional acting groups began to perform in the Southwest prior to the 1845 war between Mexico and the United States, and some California seaport towns were known to have established professional houses producing Spanish-language plays. Critic John Brokaw has traced the history of one extremely active professional troupe that toured northern Mexico and the U.S. Southwest from 1849 through 1924.[6] Theater historian Nicolás Kanellos cites seven known professional touring companies performing in the Los Angeles and San Francisco areas in the 1860s and 1870s, and around 1900 there were major Spanish-language companies all along the Mexican border, in a circuit from Laredo, Texas, to San Antonio and El Paso, through New Mexico and Arizona to Los Angeles, then north to San Francisco or south to San Diego.[7] In the latter half of the nineteenth century there was considerable activity of a somewhat different sort as Mexican groups known as *carpas* (tent shows), offering performances in the vaudeville style, toured the Rio Grande Valley. Tomás Ybarra-Frausto has characterized them as "raggle-taggle troupes" who performed "brief topical sketches and condensed versions of folk drama, intermingled with poetic recitations, music and dance." He goes on to describe theater in large towns where

the *Chicanada* [Chicano people] was entertained in the early part of this [20th] century by *tandas de variedad* [variety shows] performed by musical theater companies. Great vaudevillians . . . acted out tales embodying the pain and beauty of Pocho [Chicano] life in the urban jungle. Dialogue was a hybrid, beautiful mixture of English, Spanish and Pachuco *caló*; the style was fluid, improvisational and spontaneous, content was mordantly satirical, often poking fun at the mechanical inhuman world of the *Gavacho*, the automaton-like white man. Integral parts of the *tandas* were indigenous folk singers . . . who sang songs of life and protest to Chicano audiences from Texas to Nueva York.[8]

Kanellos gives tent theaters a great deal of credit for their influence on contemporary Chicano theater. He reports that they

continued their perennial odysseies into the [1950s], often setting up right in the camps of migrant farm laborers. . . . It is these traveling theatres that were in part responsible for giving a first exposure of the Hispanic theatrical tradition to some of the young people that would create a Chicano theatre in the late [1960s].[9]

During the 1910 revolution in Mexico many theater companies fled the war and performed in the United States, especially in Texas, where some towns were fortunate enough to have their own permanent repertory theater. During and after the revolution *carpas* toured both sides of the border, frequently improvising characters and/or themes to reflect local tastes. Professional theaters were built in many places for the exclusive purpose of performing Spanish-language plays.[10] By around 1930 the two cities with largest Hispanic populations, Los Angeles and San Antonio, had dozens of professional theater houses, some of which remained in existence for many years, others with short life spans. Many performed plays written by local writers in addition to the classics from Spain. Kanellos says that while "Spanish drama and *zarzuelas* [short musical sketches] dominated the stage up to the early twenties, the clamor for plays written by Mexican writers had increased to such an extent that by 1923 Los Angeles had

THEATER

become a center for Mexican playwrighting probably unparalleled in the history of Hispanic communities in the United States."[11] He names four Los Angeles playwrights who were popular from 1922 to 1933: Eduardo Carrillo, Adalberto Elías González, Esteban V. Escalante, and Gabriel Navarro. These are but a few of the leading names, and many other writers also saw their works produced. Kanellos calls González the most prolific and best known, and his most famous play, *Los Amores de Ramona* (The Loves of Ramona), an adaptation of Helen Hunt Jackson's immensely popular novel *Ramona* (1884), "broke all box-office records when it was seen by more than fifteen thousand people after only eight performances."[12]

A theatrical form akin to the modern revue, the *revista*, was widely performed and frequently took jabs at U.S. culture, society, and politics. A stock comic figure, the *pelado* (raggedy fellow), in the tradition of the Spanish Golden Age *gracioso* (comic sidekick) became popular because of his sense of humor, satirical remarks, and kinship with the underdog. Kanellos notes that the critical commentary of the *revista* could be successfully carried off without fear of retribution because the performances were in Spanish "and in-group sentiments could easily be expressed, especially through the protection of satire and humor."[13] The majority of the plays written and performed prior to 1965 were in Spanish.

It should be mentioned that Chicano theater was not limited to the Southwest; there was also some activity in the Midwest, in urban areas such as Chicago, beginning around the 1920s, thus reflecting the growth of the Hispanic population in other areas of the country.[14] But historically, as is the case today, the vast majority of Mexican-American plays were written and performed in the southwestern states.

Given the evidence in this brief summary, it can be fairly stated that Chicano theater is not strictly a modern phenomenon; it has a lengthy history. From the days of the conquerors there was much theater in Spanish-speaking areas of the United States, but the post-1965 period marks the first time that dramatic performances really moved out of the Spanish-speaking community and attracted more than passing attention from Anglos. All accounts of modern Chicano theater begin with the year 1965, invoke the name of Luis Valdez, and concentrate on the activities of El Teatro Campesino. This man and this troupe literally gave birth to contemporary Chicano drama and devised a form, the *acto* or skit, principally as a theatrical vehicle for voicing social and political protest. Valdez initially created his plays to instruct and entertain agricultural workers on strike against grape growers in Delano, California, in 1965. As he wrote later, he felt that the "nature of Chicanismo calls for a revolutionary turn in the arts as well as in society. Chicano theater must be revolutionary in technique as well as content. It must be popular, subject to no other critics except the pueblo [people] itself; but it must educate the pueblo toward an appreciation of *social change*, on and off the stage."[15]

THEATER

Critic Francisco Jiménez, in his article "Dramatic Principles of the Teatro Campesino," summarized the five main objectives of the original company:

1) To serve as the voice of the barrios, the community of the oppressed, 2) to inform the Chicano of the negative conditions that exist to oppress him, 3) to politicize the Chicano so he can overcome the existing conditions of oppression, 4) to inform the Chicano of his rich heritage so as to instill in him pride in his culture, and 5) to strengthen the Chicano's heart by communicating spiritual values such as love, hope and kindness.[16]

Himself a son of migrant workers, Luis Valdez was born in 1940 and became interested in theater at an early age. In spite of sporadic education—the result of his family's many moves—he earned a scholarship to attend San Jose College in California, where he studied English and dramatic literature. Later, as he worked with the San Francisco Mime Troupe, he gained experience in improvisational theater after the fashion of the Italian Renaissance commedia dell'arte. The *actos* he developed for El Teatro Campesino are improvisational— short, funny, and with a punch—filled with social and political commentary. Frequently an *acto* was a collaborative effort, the work of all the actors in the company rather than a single author. Its peculiar dramatic convention is that it, like its audience, is bilingual or even trilingual, and has ready-made dramatic irony for treating matters well known to Chicanos. The *acto* requires little in the way of scenery, costumes, or props, and is thus very mobile. (Mobility is a significant feature if the theatrical group is following strikers.) Scripts are sketchy and can be modified to suit most occasions and/or audiences. According to Valdez, the original *actos* were designed with the following five goals:

1) inspire the audience to social action;
2) illuminate specific points about social problems;
3) satirize the opposition;
4) show or hint at a solution;
5) express what people are feeling.[17]

Actos are, in effect, modern morality plays, with grape growers or other Anglo economic or political figures as forces of evil; in juxtaposition are honest and industrious farm workers as forces of good.

Almost all *actos* are humorous or satirical in nature. Valdez has explained his initial use of comedy as

stemming from a necessary situation—the necessity of lifting the morale of our strikers, who have been on strike for seventeen months. When they go to a meeting it's long and drawn out, so we do comedy with the intention of making them laugh—but with a purpose. We try to make social points, not in spite of the comedy, but through it. This leads us into satire and slapstick, and sometimes very close to the underlying tragedy of it all—the fact that human

beings have been wasted in farm labor for
generations.[18]

Director and critic Jorge Huerta has best summarized
the role and importance of the language of Chicano
theater:

> The Chicano is basically bilingual, and his every act
> reflects that duality. In many instances, Chicanos speak
> a third, subculture language, *caló*, which has
> developed in barrios all around the country to give
> each region its own peculiar idioms and phrases. The
> first problem a non-Chicano encounters viewing a
> *teatro* performance is this "trilingualism"—even people
> who have studied Spanish as a foreign language have
> difficulty following the quick transitions from English
> to Spanish to *caló*. When we analyze *actos* we have
> entered the realm of Chicano culture in no uncertain
> terms, and must be prepared to follow closely the
> double entendres and non-translatable phrases which
> give Chicano theatre its unique flavor.[19]

Among the famous *actos* devised by Valdez and first
performed by El Teatro Campesino are *Las Dos Caras del
Patroncito* (The Two Faces of the Boss), a 1965 work critical of the grape growers, and *La Quinta Temporada* (The
Fifth Season), produced in 1966 and focusing on the
labor contractor. *La Conquista de México* (The Conquest
of Mexico), first produced in 1968, was a puppet show
demonstrating the similarities between the Spanish
conquest of Mexico and the *gringo* conquest of Chica-

nos. One of the oldest and perhaps the best-known example of an *acto* is *Los Vendidos* (The Sellouts), written by Luis Valdez and first performed in 1967. It is set in Honest Sancho's Used Mexican Lot and Mexican Curio Shop, where Miss Jiménez (she pronounces it "Jimmynez," a distinctly "American sounding" name) arrives in search of a token Mexican to work in the governor's office. Sancho demonstrates several stereotypical models, including the farm worker, the *pachuco* or urban gangster, the revolutionary, and finally the much-desired middle-class Mexican-American. Miss Jiménez rejects all but the last, finding him the only one acceptable because he has embraced Anglo-American values so fully that he has completely denied his heritage, thus becoming a *vendido*. As the play closes, however, the audience sees that the true purpose of the business is to supply Chicano activists who, in disguise, infiltrate all segments of Anglo society. Sancho turns out to be a robot, and the other "models" come to life and reveal their humanness and purpose. It is a humorous play treating the serious problems of cultural assimilation, the abuse of workers, and racial and ethnic stereotypes.

In addition to their support of farm workers El Teatro Campesino in the early years also toured college and university campuses to earn money and to spread its dramatic message. Later there was a national tour, including performances in New York and another in Washington, DC, on the steps of the Capitol for the subcommittee on migrant labor. As a result of the New

York work, the troupe received an Obie Award and an invitation to participate in 1967 at the Théâtre des Nations in Nancy, France.

As the Teatro grew and moved to Del Rey and later San Juan Bautista, it also developed other theatrical forms, broadening its themes to include all aspects of Chicano existence. El Centro Campesino Cultural (the Workers' Cultural Center) emerged in 1967 as an outgrowth of the theater. This complex, located in San Juan Bautista, became a significant center for dissemination not only of theater but also music, art, and other manifestations of Chicano culture. The theater, in Valdez's words, was becoming

more concerned with the broad sweep of history that the Chicano was caught up in, the international struggle by working class people all over the world, the effect of U.S. imperialism on Vietnam, Latin America, Asia, etc.
. . . We saw the Chicano as part of a total thrust by humanity struggling toward something, a new world, a new society. A new vision of mankind.[20]

Some of the new themes are reflected in the *actos*. *No Saco Nada de la Escuela* (I Don't Get Anything Out of School) is a 1969 piece which presents the problems of the Chicano in the English-language, Anglo-dominated school system. *Vietnam Campesino* (Vietnam Farm worker) of 1970 and *Soldado Razo* (Chicano Soldier) of the following year are antiwar plays with a Chicano perspective.

After establishing a headquarters in San Juan Bautista in 1971, Luis Valdez and his troupe began writing and performing another theater form unique to Chicano theatre, the *mito* or myth. Valdez characterized the *mito* in 1973:

The FORM of our mitos is evolving from
something-resembling-a-play to
something-that-feels-like-ritual. At the center of our
mitos so far (as opposed to the ACTOS) is a story. A
parable (parábula) that unravels like a flower
indo-fashion to reveal the total significance of a certain
event. And that vision of totality is what truly defines
a mito. In other words, the CONTENT of a mito is the
Indo Vision of the Universe. And that vision is
religious, as well as political, cultural, social, personal,
etc. It is total.[21]

Mitos go beyond the principally political *actos* and include themes such as history, religion, and legend. Among the *mitos* are *Dark Root of a Scream*, also about the Vietnam war, and *Bernabé*, the story of a village idiot who wishes to marry La Tierra, the Earth. He is a symbol of mankind's lost love for the planet, and he must be sacrificed in order for harmony to be restored with the Sun, the chief god of the Aztecs.

Another theatrical form El Teatro Campesino has experimented with is the *corrido* (ballad), which reflects the popularity of stories set to music in the Mexican-American community. Music had always played a role in the *actos*, but in the *corrido* it is central, for the play

THEATER

tells a story to music as actors mime the events described. There may also be dance or narration which blends with the music to make a cultural or political statement. Other Chicano theater companies have also performed *corridos*. The Teatro de la Gente's *Corrido de Juan Endrogado* (The Ballad of Juan Drugged), one of the genre's most famous, is about a Chicano youth who dies as a result of his experiences with drugs. He comes back as a spirit, dressed in the traditional Uncle Sam suit, and kills his supplier. The play has a narrator/balladeer who interprets and describes the scene, and the music is appropriate to the action.

El Teatro Campesino's first full-length play was *La carpa de los Rasquachis* (The Tent of the Underdogs), sometimes called *La gran carpa de los Rasquachis* (The Big Tent . . .). This 1974 work presents the experiences of Jesús Pelado Rasquachi, a Mexican who comes to the United States with high hopes for fortune but encounters only misery and death. It mixes Christian and Mexican Indian tales and employs music, dance, and ritual. Jorge Huerta describes *La carpa* as combining the *acto, corrido, mito*, and *commedia* into a flowing whole.[22] *La carpa* was a huge success, with a national tour of the United States and two tours in Europe. Valdez adapted it for National Public Television in 1976 and gave it the title *El Corrido*. In this form it was seen by millions of people, making it the most visible Chicano play since the beginnings of El Teatro Campesino in 1965.

Other full-length plays by Valdez include *The Shrunken Head of Pancho Villa* and *I Don't Have to Show*

UNDERSTANDING CHICANO LITERATURE

You No Stinking Badges. The former is about a Chicano boy, Joaquín, who is sent to reform school because of the trouble he causes in school. When he returns home in the last act, he is well dressed and well behaved, but he has no head. The play is a strong cry against assimilation and a call for action in the education of Chicanos. *Badges* is a four-character play whose title comes from a Mexican bandit's challenge to Humphrey Bogart's character in the movie *The Treasure of the Sierra Madre*, based on the B. Traven novel. This play departs from the author's early work in that the family represented here is from the middle class. The parents (Connie and Buddy) are Chicano actors who play minor roles in movies, usually as domestics, gardeners, or prostitutes. Their son (Sonny) is a dropout from Harvard Law School, a troubled young man, unsure of his identity. He also wishes to be an actor, but has been rejected by the Hollywood community which doesn't want "Mexicans" in leading roles. He attacks his parents for taking roles representing popular stereotypes. He threatens suicide and the murder of his parents and his Japanese-American girlfriend. Along with this serious theme *Badges* is frequently humorous. With its characterization of life in the United States as a situation comedy it has been called a metaphor of life as television. The play had a successful run in 1986 at the Los Angeles Theatre Center.

While El Teatro Campesino was, and still is, the largest and best-known theater group,[23] it by no means stands alone. There were many small groups in commu-

THEATER

nities throughout the Southwest in the 1960s, so many in fact that El Teatro Campesino decided to hold a national theater festival in 1970. This led in 1971 to the founding of TENAZ, an acronym for *El Teatro Nacional de Aztlán* (The National Theatre of Aztlán). TENAZ was responsible for coordination and communication of theater activities; it also established a series of summer workshops for members. Summer workshops have been held most years since, and membership has grown to over seventy-five theaters, including—to name but a few present and former groups—Teatro Aztlán (Northridge, California), Teatro de los Barrios (San Antonio), Teatro de los Estudiantes (Ann Arbor, Michigan), Teatro Popular del Barrio (San Diego), Teatro Rasquachi (Colorado Springs), Teatro Libertad (Tucson), and Teatro Desengaño del Pueblo, (Gary–East Chicago).

One of the most prominent of the other early Chicano companies was El Teatro de la Esperanza (The Theatre of Hope), founded in July of 1971 by Jorge Huerta, one of contemporary Chicano theater's most active and respected directors and critics. In 1973 Huerta edited a collection of eight of his troupe's works and published them under the title *El Teatro de la Esperanza*. These plays are in the same vein as the *mitos* and *actos* of El Teatro Campesino. Another significant piece by El Teatro de la Esperanza is a collective one, *Guadalupe*, which was performed on a tour in 1974 in California and Mexico and later filmed for television in Mexico City for a nationwide broadcast. The play is based on events that took place in 1972 in the small California town of Guadalupe, during a period when Chicano residents met as a committee to attempt to improve their living conditions and to better their children's schools. The controlling interests in town arrested several committee members, putting some in jail. In 1973 the California State Advisory Commission on Civil Rights issued a report documenting oppression in the town. Huerta's play was developed from interviews with townspeople and included music, scenes of police brutality, church and civic oppression, and the effects of alcohol and drugs. Huerta described the play and its reception in great detail in "From the Temple to the Arena: Teatro Chicano Today," and concluded:

Unlike the early actos of the Teatro Campesino, "Guadalupe" could not call for simple solutions. There were more problems being exposed, and though each was different from the other, still they were inter-related. . . . Even as the Teatro de la Esperanza was creating its obra (work), the group realized that there were no easy solutions and that their major purpose would be in exposing the problems and hoping the communities would take some sort of action. That seems the least a political theatre can hope for.[24]

As Huerta's words attest, his theater group and others of the 60s and early 70s were exposing social ills in hopes of spurring their audiences to political action.

THEATER

Many of the early plays were collective efforts, frequently improvised and not written down until weeks or months after they were performed, if at all. With the goals mainly social and political, the impact of Chicano theater was intended to be immediate, with a live audience, and the words were not designed for reading or for solitary contemplation at a later time. As a consequence, only a very few were published. As time passed, however, more Chicanos developed a greater interest in theater and grew more skillful as actors and directors; it is only natural that some would turn to composing individual plays, and that outstanding playwrights would soon attempt to see their work in print. It is also natural that the theater would eventually evolve to include treatments of matters unrelated to contemporary social and political Chicano problems.

Nephtalí de León, a poet and writer of children's literature, published a collection of drama in 1972. The works in *Five Plays* are bilingual and follow El Teatro Campesino's lead in that they treat common Chicano social themes. The first, *The Death of Ernesto Nerios*, is based on an actual police shooting of a young Chicano in Lubbock, Texas, in 1971. Ernesto, a Vietnam veteran facing poverty, family illness, and the possible loss of his job, is shot following an argument with a store clerk. The play deals with misfortune and injustice, but also with the element of the supernatural in all peoples' lives. *Chicanos! The Living and the Dead* is like El Teatro Campesino's *No Saco Nada de la Escuela* in that it deals with Chicano grievances against the Anglo school systems. The "Dead" of the title are Che Guevara of the Cuban revolution and Rubén Salazar, Chicano journalist killed during the 1970 Chicano moratorium against the Vietnam war. Both figures appear in one scene and speak on behalf of the earth's downtrodden. The play ends with a plea for love and tolerance, but with a warning that educational reforms are overdue. *Play Number 9* draws on Greek mythology by equating the Chicano with Prometheus, who was enchained for stealing the secret of fire from the gods, while the Chicano is culturally, socially, and economically enchained because the American education system has not met his needs. In *The Judging of Man* the earth has been destroyed by war; allegorical characters—Death, Destiny, Beauty, Faith, and Virtue—argue over which has absolute claims on Mankind. Destiny prevails as de León closes his play on a note of hope and peace for everyone. *The Flies* is a comedy popular with audiences, but it too has a dark side. It is about three fly friends, two males and one female, and the death of one of the males. Behind the amusing dialogue is the message that Chicano people are just as vulnerable to human cruelty as are the protagonists of the play—all victims of the actions of dominant forces.

Carlos Morton is another Chicano playwright who has enjoyed success in presenting his plays and in obtaining their publication. His first effort, *Desolation Car Lot*, was produced in 1973 at the University of Texas, El Paso, as part of a Mexican Independence Day celebration. He published *El Jardín* (The Garden) in 1974, then traveled briefly with El Teatro Campesino. In addition to further theater experience in 1976 with the University of California at San Diego, he worked with the San Francisco Mime Troupe in 1979 as a playwright-in-residence. Huerta has characterized Morton as a

wandering playwright whose plays have been produced . . . from coast to coast. No other playwright besides Luis Valdez has been as active and prolific as Carlos Morton. He might be termed a one-man teatro, expressing a vision of the Chicano that is informed by his own experiences and his observations of the world around him.[25]

In 1983 Arte Público Press issued a collection of four of Morton's plays which had previously appeared individually in journals. *The Many Deaths of Danny Rosales* includes the title play, *Rancho Hollywood*, *Los Dorados* (The Golden Ones), and *El Jardín*. The last is a farce, a parody of the fall of man, but with a Chicano twist, as Eve complains about eating beans, and the serpent refers to her as his "little enchilada." *Los Dorados* is a view of a century and a half of the history of Mexicans in the United States. *Rancho Hollywood* is a satirical comedy about the stereotypical presentations of Latinos in television and motion pictures. The title piece, winner of the Hispanic Playwrights Festival Award, New York Shakespeare Festival, is Morton's most famous work. It concerns the trial of an Anglo police chief, Fred Hall, accused of the shotgun slaying of a Chicano, Danny

Rosales. The crime is revealed through flashbacks en-
acted during the cross-examination. Hall is found guilty
of aggravated assault and receives a sentence of two to
ten years in prison. Rosales's wife, Berta, is fined $49.50
for some things she did after her husband's death. She
reacts with a listing of Danny's many deaths: once
when he was born poor, once when he didn't get a
decent education, once with a shotgun, once with a
pick and shovel, and, finally, once in a court of law. As
the play closes, it is revealed that the Hall family (the
wife and daughter had aided in the burial and were
thus accomplices after the fact) were two years later
found guilty of violating Danny's civil rights. *The Many
Deaths of Danny Rosales* is based on an actual event, and
the playwright's staging of the action in a documentary
fashion gives the work a hard-edged reality. It is a vivid,
bitter portrayal of the Chicano's perception of the justice he can expect in the Anglo court system.

Another of Morton's plays, *Pancho Diablo*, is the
story of the Devil, who escaped to earth after growing
disgusted with hell. God, in disguise, goes to Texas,
where he finds Pancho working as an undertaker. This
farce, with music and in the *corrido* tradition, was performed during New York City's Festival Latino in the
summer of 1987.

Among Rubén Sierra's best plays is *La raza pura o
Racial, Racial* (The Pure Race or Racial, Racial). It is a
comical satire about the purity of race in America, depicting the conflict faced by an Anglo girl and a
Mexican-American boy in their new love. It is like *Los*

Vendidos in that it takes place in the "All-Purpose Racial Agency," which has a complete array of models ranging in shades from "Chicano Cream" through "Acapulco Gold." *Manolo*, a three-act play with an epilogue, treats the drug problems of a returned Vietnam veteran. This work provides a strikingly realistic picture of life in a Chicano *barrio* and, because it is mostly in English, is accessible to an Anglo audience. In 1982 Huerta called *Manolo* one of the "few successfully written and produced realistic Chicano plays that has been published to date, and it merits the attention of any study of serious Chicano drama."[26] Sierra's still unpublished plays include *The Conquering Father*, a one-act allegory about God, time, and religion, and *La capirotada de los espejos* (The Conglomeration of Mirrors), which is concerned with Chicano history. *The Millionaire y el pobrecito* (The Millionaire and the Poor Child) is an adaptation of Mark Twain's *The Prince and the Pauper* with a rich Anglo and a poor Chicano exchanging places in life. *I Am Celso*, which Sierra wrote with Jorge Huerta, was adapted from poetry written by Leo Romero.

Fausto Avedaño published *El corrido de California* (The Ballad of California) in 1979. This is a historical piece treating the 1846 American military invasion of California with the focus on a Mexican family. Don Gerónimo, the mayor of a small town, tries to remain neutral, while his son, Rafael, resists the foreign invasion. The play ends with John C. Calhoun pleading with the U.S. Senate to depart from the doctrine of Manifest Destiny and reject the incorporation of the

UNDERSTANDING CHICANO LITERATURE

Southwest into the Union. *El corrido de California* is another manifestation of Chicano literature's close relationship with Chicano history.

While Nephtalí de León, Carlos Morton, and others have treated contemporary social and political themes, some dramatists have turned to other matters. For example, Estela Portillo Trambley, poet and short story writer as well as dramatist, wrote *The Day of the Swallows* (1971), a full-length play in three acts about a lesbian relationship. Josefa, the protagonist, is a bitter woman who has suffered much because of her treatment by men; in order to keep her relationship with an ex-prostitute secret, she mutilates a young male witness to her affair, an act which eventually drives her to suicide. The play is realistic, with rich imagery, fine language, and a homosexual theme rarely treated in Chicano literature—an element which has restricted its appeal. Portillo Trambley, one of the few women playwrights to see her work in printed form, has also published *Sun Images* and a collection, *Sor Juana and Other Plays*. *Sor Juana* is a historical piece, presenting an episode in the life of Sor Juana Inés de la Cruz, one of Mexico's most celebrated writers and feminist thinkers. *Blacklight* portrays the disintegration of a Chicano family living in a border town. The play combines the real, miserable existence of contemporary wetbacks with images of the past, as Aztec gods also appear on stage. *Blacklight* was a second-place winner in the 1985 Latin American Theatre Festival in New York City. Portillo Trambley's plays have been produced in many places, including Texas, New Mexico, California, and Mexico.

Perhaps the Chicano play best known to Anglo audiences to date is a musical by Luis Valdez, *Zoot Suit.* After a long and successful run in California it became the first play by a Chicano to be performed on a Broadway stage (Winter Garden Theater, beginning in March 1979). Although it did not enjoy a lengthy Broadway run, *Zoot Suit* is significant because it is a social and political play, based on the *acto* form. It includes elements of the *mito* and the *corrido*, and it has been performed outside Chicano or academic circles with all America for an audience. The author based his work on the true events surrounding the Los Angeles Sleepy Lagoon Murder of 1942 and the racial confrontations of the following year. Writer Richard Rodriguez has summarized the actual history of some of the events depicted in Valdez's creation:

In 1943 American sailors in Los Angeles ventured into an evil vein of boredom which led to the east side of town where they beat up barrio teenagers who were dressed in the burlesque pink costume of the day. The "Zoot Suit Riots" lasted for several nights. City officials fell asleep early, and the Los Angeles press encouraged the high-spirited sailors.[27]

Zoot Suit's main character, the *pachuco*, is a stylized representation of one of the first Mexican-Americans to exhibit pride in his complex origins, and the first to resist conformity either to his Mexican or to his Anglo heritage. Octavio Paz, noted Mexican writer, commented on the *pachucos* as early as 1950, describing them as

youths, for the most part of Mexican origin, who form gangs in Southern cities; they can be identified by their language and behavior as well as by the clothing they affect. They are instinctive rebels, and North American racism has vented its wrath on them more than once. But the *pachucos* do not attempt to vindicate their race or the nationality of their forebears. Their attitude reveals an obstinate, almost fanatical will-to-be, but this will affirms nothing specific except their determination—it is an ambiguous one . . . —not to be like those around them. The *pachuco* does not want to become a Mexican again; at the same time he does not want to blend into the life of North America. His whole being is sheer negative impulse, a tangle of contradictions, an enigma.[28]

The story line of *Zoot Suit* is uncomplicated: Henry Reyna and his companions are arrested for killing another Chicano. Their conviction in a mass trial is a travesty of justice, with the press playing an important role as a villain. George and Alice, lawyer and social crusader, manage a successful appeal, but the pardoned Chicanos still must return to a world which has no place for them. The riots, instigated by the press, take place at the same time as the trial. Anglo soldiers and sailors cruise the *barrios*, beating up anyone they encounter dressed in a zoot suit. The character of the *pachuco* is the play's conscience. In a manifestation of

THEATER

self-conscious theater he is always present, commenting on the action, needling the characters, chiding the audience for taking the play too seriously, or chiding Henry for not taking it seriously enough. While Henry is the protagonist, *El Pachuco*, his alter ego, is a living myth, the personification of a Chicano striving to assert his identity, wanting to be himself and to earn respect on his own terms, not those dictated by others.

Zoot Suit did not meet with critical success in its Broadway run, with some critics faulting the play for its theme and others for its style. Still others cited racism as a cause for the play's poor showing, with accusations that the New York theater was rigidly segregated. But the Los Angeles run of the play had been a huge critical and popular success, with 46 weeks of performances and combined audiences of more than 400,000.[29] The facts that this work was so well received in California, among Chicanos, and that (for whatever reasons) it did not fare well on the east coast, bring up serious questions concerning the current state and the future direction of all Chicano drama.

Currently Chicano theater is in transition. After the vibrant, intense, sociopolitical movement of the 1960s and early 1970s, drama in the 1980s has become more established and has, therefore, changed direction. As Nicolás Kanellos observed,

the days of *teatro* as an arm of revolutionary nationalism are over. The revolutionary aims of the movement have resulted in modest reforms and certain accommodations. Luis Valdez now sits on the California Arts Council. Many other *teatro* and former *teatro* people are members of local arts agencies and boards throughout the Southwest. Former *teatristas* are now professors of drama, authors, and editors of scholarly books and journals on Chicano literature and theatre.[30]

According to Kanellos, acting troupes once toured the country performing without payment for political organizations, but now most present their works only on college campuses and charge fees, sometimes very large ones:

Perhaps the academy is a place where Chicano theater may be pursued and developed as an art form until such a time when it will be ready to compete successfully on the Anglo-dominated national scene. Whatever the motivation, the academy has fostered the second stage in the development of *teatro*. In this stage, professional artistry is as important as the sociopolitical message. In this way, the previously restrictive nationalism can give way to an openness, where influences and directions outside of the grass roots culture can be encouraged.[31]

Chicano theater is no different from any other theater in that it requires an audience for its existence. During the early days the audience was a captive one, and common Chicano problems provided subjects for the playwright and an inherent dramatic irony prompted great spectator response. The national political conservatism of the 1980s has changed the environment for Chicano theater, and the very modest economic and social advancements made by many Chicano people have altered the audiences; increasingly they are populated by members of the middle class. The bilingual and bicultural nature of much of this theater restricts the audience, so that the large majority of Anglos, even the most avid theatergoers, stand to miss a great deal of what is said on stage; after seeing a Chicano play or two, those who do not understand the language are not likely to see another. Because theater is the most immediate of the literary arts (it is alive), it requires an immediate audience, and that audience dictates theatrical success or failure. There are excellent Chicano playwrights who must respond to the changing nature of their audiences, because to fail to do so would spell doom for their livelihood and for Chicano theater. Four hundred years of theater history have proven that Chicano drama has responded to countless changes in the past; although the challenges it faces today are huge, it is responding to new audiences and to new situations, and continues to be a fascinating and unique facet of Chicano literature.

Notes

1. See Richard E. Leinaweaver, "*Rabinal Achí:* Commentary," and "*Rabinal Achí:* English Translation," *Latin American Theatre Review* 1, 2 (Spring 1968): 3–54.

UNDERSTANDING CHICANO LITERATURE

2. See Willis Knapp Jones, *Behind Spanish American Footlights* (Austin: University of Texas Press, 1966), esp. ch. 31, "Mexico's Theatre over 375 Years."

3. For discussion and translation, see T. M. Pearce, "Los Moros y los Cristianos: Early American Play," *New Mexico Folklore Record 2* (1947–48): 59–69.

4. John E. Englekirk, "Notes on the Repertoire of the New Mexico Spanish Folk Theatre," *Southwestern Folklore Quarterly* 4 (1940): 227.

5. See Aureliano M. Espinosa and J. Manuel Espinosa, "The Texans,," *New Mexican Quarterly Review* 13 (1943): 299–308.

6. John W. Brokaw, "A Mexican-American Acting Company, 1849–1924," *Educational Theatre Journal 17* (Mar. 1975): 23–29.

7. Nicolás Kanellos, *Two Centuries of Hispanic Theatre in the Southwest.* (Houston: Revista Chicano-Riqueña, 1982) 6.

8. Tomás Ybarra-Frausto, "Puntos de Partida," *Latin American Theatre Review* 4, 2 (Spring 1971): 52.

9. Kanellos, 18.

10. For an example see Armando Miguélez, "El Teatro Carmen (1915–1923): Centro del Arte Escénico Hispano en Tucson," *Mexican American Theatre: Then and Now*, ed. Nicolás Kanellos (Houston: Arte Público Press, 1983) 52–67.

11. Kanellos, *Two Centuries* 9–10.

12. Kanellos, *Two Centuries* 15.

13. Kanellos, *Two Centuries* 17.

14. See Nicolás Kanellos, "Fifty Years of Theatre in the Latino Communities of Northwest Indiana," *Mexican American Theatre: Legacy and Reality* (Pittsburgh: Latin American Literary Review Press, 1987) 63–75.

15. Luis Valdez, *Actos: El Teatro Campesino* (San Juan Bautista, CA: La Cucaracha Press, 1971) 2.

16. Francisco Jiménez, "Dramatic Principles of the Teatro Campesino", *The Bilingual Review/La Revista Bilingüe* 2, 1–2 (Jan.-Aug. 1975): 101–02.

17. Valdez 6.

18. Quoted Jiménez 102.

THEATER

19. Jorge A. Huerta, "Chicano Agit-Prop: The Early *Actos* of El Teatro Campesino," *Latin American Theatre Review* 10, 2 (Spring 1977): 46–47.

20. *El Teatro Campesino: The First Twenty Years.* (San Juan Bautista, CA: El Teatro Campesino, 1985) 11.

21. Luis Valdez, "Notes on Chicano Theatre," *Chicano Theatre One* (San Juan Bautista: La Cucaracha Press, 1973) 7.

22. Jorge A. Huerta, *Chicano Theatre: Themes and Forms* (Ypsilanti, MI: Bilingual Press/Editorial Bilingüe, 1982) 200.

23. The University of California at Santa Barbara is the home of the archives of Luis Valdez and El Teatro Campesino. A special collection, part of the Colección Tloque Nahuaque, contains unpublished scripts, letters, articles, reviews, photographs, posters, art, records, and films.

24. Jorge A. Huerta, "From the Temple to the Arena: Teatro Chicano Today," *The Identification and Analysis of Chicano Literature*, ed. Francisco Jiménez. (New York: Bilingual Press/Editorial Bilingüe, 1979) 106.

25. Huerta, *Chicano Theatre* 169.

26. Huerta, *Chicano Theatre* 116.

27. Richard Rodriguez, "Mexico's Children," *The American Scholar* Spring 1986: 165.

28. Octavio Paz, *The Labyrinth of Solitude: Life and Thought in Mexico* (New York: Grove Press, 1961) 14. Originally published in 1950 by *Cuadernos Americanos*, Mexico. Revised and expanded in 1959 for Fondo de Cultura Económica, Mexico. Spanish title: *El laberinto de la soledad.*

29. *Zoot Suit* was made into a commercial film (1981), directed by Valdez and starring Edward James Olmos, Daniel Valdez (Luis's brother) and Tyne Daly. Another film written and directed by Luis Valdez was a large box-office success in the summer of 1987. *La Bamba,*

starring Lou Diamond Phillips and Esai Morales, presents the story of 1950s rock music star Ritchie Valens, the first Chicano to become a popular singer nationwide. His hit song, "La Bamba," based on a Mexican folk dance, was the first Spanish-language rock and roll success.

30. Nicolás Kanellos, "Chicano Theatre," *Chicano Literature: A Reference Guide*, ed. Julio A. Martínez and Francisco A. Lomelí (Westport, CT: Greenwood Press, 1985) 182.

31. Kanellos, "Chicano Theatre" 182–83.

CHAPTER 3

Novel

Most critics agree that the first modern Chicano novel is *Pocho*, published in 1959 by California-born José Antonio Villarreal. Since that time the genre has grown and developed rapidly as readers and critics outside as well as inside the Chicano community are beginning to discover the most prominent novelists. It is important to note that Chicano prose fiction did not spring forth fully grown in the middle years of this century; it has deep roots, with many little-known but highly talented writers practicing their craft over the course of several centuries.

The groundwork for modern Chicano prose was laid as soon as the Spanish publicized their presence in the New World. The earliest extant examples of writings from the North American continent are the many chronicles of the Spanish explorers of the present-day southwestern United States. In addition to this large body of written historical literature there is a long tradition in the Southwest of oral folk literature, mostly of anonymous origin, with Spanish and Mexican tales handed down from generation to generation, many still heard today.

Aside from folktales, historical narratives, diaries, and the like, there was no other literary prose in the American Southwest until about the second half of the nineteenth century. It was during this period that many Spanish-language newspapers were established, providing writers with a place to publish their literary efforts. Around the end of the nineteenth century several important prose writers published their work in book form for the first time. Two examples are Eusebio Chacón (1869–1948) and Miguel Antonio Otero (1859–1944). Chacón issued two short novels in 1892: *El hijo de la tempestad* (Child of the Storm) and *Tras la tormenta la calma* (The Calm after the Storm). Otero's three-volume autobiography (*My Life on the Frontier 1865–1882*), in English, is an accurate literary portrait of frontier life in the Southwest in the second half of the century. It contains information about the author from the age of five until 1906, the end of his eight-year career as governor of the New Mexico Territory. It is rich with descriptions of the land and images of famous American legends such as Wild Bill Hickok and Billy the Kid.

Another New Mexican, Felipe Maximiliano Chacón (1873–?), wrote only one short (183 pages) volume in Spanish, published in 1924: *Obras de Felipe Maximiliano Chacón, El Cantor Neomexicano: Poesía y Prosa* (Works of Felipe Maximiliano Chacón, the New Mexican Bard: Poetry and Prose). Chacón was a newspaper editor and

NOVEL

writer who managed *La Bandera Americana* (The American Flag), a popular Albuquerque paper. His prose consists of a 30-page novelette and two short pieces; the best effort, "Don Julio Berlanga," is an account of the experiences of a Las Vegas, New Mexico, cowhand in 1918. This work has received praise for its language and style as well as for its authentic reflection of Mexican-American life of the time.

One highly significant early novel was issued in Los Angeles in 1928 by Daniel Venegas, founder and editor of *El Malcriado* (The Brat), a weekly satirical newspaper. *Las aventuras de Don Chipote o Cuando los pericos mamen* (The Adventures of Don Chipote or When Parakeets May Suckle Their Young) was recently rediscovered by scholar Nicolás Kanellos, who supervised a reprint in 1984. The novel is a humorous account of a Mexican immigrant, Don Chipote, who journeys throughout the southwestern United States. His wife soon follows, searching for her wayward spouse. She finally catches up with him in a Los Angeles theater, and they return to Mexico because "Mexicans will only become rich in the United States when parakeets suckle their young."

In this picaresque tale the author criticizes U.S. treatment of Mexican and Chicano workers, both rural and urban. Venegas is among the first writers to employ the *caló* dialect of the Mexican-Americans, thus reflecting a linguistic realism not previously encountered. In a 1984 article Kanellos called *Don Chipote* "a rich repository of the Chicano lexicon," and accurately described the author as a forerunner of such masterful contemporary novelists as Tomás Rivera, Rolando Hinojosa, and Miguel Méndez.[1]

In addition to prose written for Spanish-language newspapers in the first few decades of the twentieth century, there were some works composed for magazines, usually in English. María Cristina Mena wrote romantic, sentimental, completely idealized and unrealistic stories which she published from 1913 to 1916, principally in the magazine *Century.* It is unfortunate that her work did much to perpetuate among Anglo readers a romanticized stereotype of Mexican-Americans. As Raymund Paredes has noted, Mena's portrayals are "ultimately obsequious, and if one can appreciate the weight of popular attitudes on Mena's consciousness, one can also say that a braver, more perceptive writer would have confronted the life of her culture more forcefully."[2] Although some writers did portray their culture more forcefully (Robert Torres in his pieces in *Esquire* magazine, or Josephina Niggli in her novel *Mexican Village,* for example), it was not until 1947 and the work by Mario Suárez that there is a writer composing in English who presents a true, realistic, unsentimental picture of Chicanos.

Suárez wrote about his people in "El Hoyo" (The Hole), a Tucson Arizona, neighborhood, and was probably the first to employ in fiction the term *Chicano.* In contrast to Mena's stereotypes, Suárez paints portraits of the *barrio* inhabitants by comparing them to a common food, a *capirotada:*

Its origin is uncertain. But it is made of old, new, stale, and hard bread. It is sprinkled with water and then it is cooked with raisins, olives, onions, tomatoes, peanuts, cheese, and general leftovers of that which is good and bad. It is seasoned with salt, sugar, pepper, and sometimes chili or tomato sauce. It is fired with tequila or sherry wine. It is served hot, cold, or just "on the weather" as they say in El Hoyo. The Garcías like it one way; the Quevedos another. While in general appearance it does not differ much from one home to another it tastes different everywhere. Nevertheless it is still *capirotada*. And so it is with El Hoyo's *chicanos*. While many seem to the undiscerning eye to be alike it is only because collectively they are referred to as *chicanos*. But like *capirotada*, fixed in a thousand ways and served on a thousand tables, which can only be evaluated by individual taste, the *chicanos* must be so distinguished.[3]

Suárez thus sets the stage for the impressive flowering of Chicano novels and short stories from the 1960s to the present, a period during which the reader sees the Chicano *capirotada* in all of its flavors, good or bad, heavily or subtly spiced, served up in a wide variety of ways.

With such a phenomenon as the contemporary Chicano novel (1959 to the present), and with such a large number of writers working at the same time, finding a reasonable and systematic framework for discussion becomes a difficult matter. This study follows a somewhat arbitrary schema, dividing the authors into three groups: 1) the early contributors, from 1959 to about 1972, a time when the first writers began to publish; 2) the most influential novelists, those who published between 1972 and 1975, years during which the most prominent emerged; 3) other writers, those who have, for various reasons, made significant contributions to the genre.

The Early Contributors

The early period begins, as it does in all studies of the contemporary Chicano novel, with *Pocho*, the landmark work by José Antonio Villarreal. It is the earliest long prose piece by a Mexican-American to be issued by a major U.S. publishing company, and it is frequently hailed for its historical value as a reflection of Mexican-American life in what is termed the "assimilationist" period in their history. In the *Bildungsroman* (novel of self-discovery) tradition, *Pocho* is the story of a young boy, Richard Rubio, and his attempt to find his place in the world. Set in pre-World War II Santa Clara, California, it portrays Richard as he grapples with common teen-age problems—parents, religion, sex, school—but with a sociocultural twist: Richard is a Chicano, who gradually discovers that this fact makes a big difference in his life. There is much conflict between Richard and his parents, as broadening cultural differences between his mother and father eventually lead to a family breakup. At the end of the novel war breaks out, and

Richard sets off to join the military. The author has stated that *Pocho* was written to "share my experiences of growing up in an old country, traditional way, breaking away from that culture and going on to a new way of life, yet still holding on to the traditional ways that were good and adding to them the new things I liked in the Anglo-American society."[4]

It is noteworthy that *Pocho,* for all of its praise as a landmark work, has frequently been controversial among Chicano critics. In an introductory essay for a 1970 paperback edition, Ramón E. Ruiz criticizes Villarreal for not making the racial conflict and prejudice portrayed in the book its central theme. This article, which Villarreal did not wish to have included with the publication, did much to set the tone for some of *Pocho*'s subsequent condemnation from the Chicano community. The author no doubt added to the problem by not adhering to the heavy rhetoric of the late 60s Chicano Movement, going so far as to state that he did not really consider himself a Chicano and to entertain the possibility that Chicano literature did not even exist. In spite of adverse reactions to the author's public statements and to his writing, *Pocho* has become a best-selling novel, with over 160,000 copies in circulation. The latest printing does not include the Ruiz introduction.

As the furor of the political movement has diminished, more critics have begun to examine the novel for its literary merit rather than its social commentary. It has had its share of negative criticism in this regard as well. Some have faulted *Pocho* for the author's attempt to duplicate Spanish language structures with English words, with a resulting artificiality and strange-sounding syntax. Others have condemned it for a lack of focus. Some have discovered and cited thematic inconsistencies. But the fact remains that *Pocho*, in spite of its shortcomings, is the quintessential Chicano novel of self-discovery, matched only by Rudolfo A. Anaya's 1972 masterpiece, *Bless Me, Última*, a vastly different work.

Villarreal has also written *The Fifth Horseman* (1974), noteworthy because it is a Chicano work set prior to the Mexican revolution of 1910, and *Clemente Chacón* (1984), in which the protagonist, unlike Richard Rubio, finally asserts his Chicano cultural identity. *The Fifth Horseman* is technically and artistically much better than *Pocho*, but it has received only limited critical attention, even after being reissued in 1984. Villarreal's second book is about Heraclio Inés, a peasant on a large ranch in northern Mexico. He is the fifth son in a family of skilled horsemen and learns that he must live by a strict code of honor. His story takes him through a love affair, a marriage, and long service in Pancho Villa's army. The author has stated in several instances that his first two books are part of a planned tetrology, with *The Houyhnhnms* and *Call Me Ishmael* as yet unpublished.

Clemente Chacón is a Chicano version of the Horatio Alger story: Ramón Alvarez, a Mexican street child, crosses to the United States, changes his name to Clemente Chacón, and later becomes a successful insur-

NOVEL

ance executive. The novel takes place during a single September day in 1972. Through dialogue and flashbacks the protagonist's history is revealed as he gropes with his cultural identity until, near the end, he proclaims: "I am a Mexican and I am an American, and there is no reason in the world why I can't be both." Technically, this is the author's best work, but it occasionally stumbles, ironically, over too much dialogue that emerges sounding like social propaganda.

Richard Vásquez is another writer of the early period whose novels have enjoyed popularity. His first, *Chicano* (1970), written in English, has subsequently appeared in Spanish and German translations. The author constructs his tale around the lives of four generations of Sandovals, Mexicans who settled in East Los Angeles. A gloomy tone permeates; from the moment of Hector Sandoval's arrival with his family in their new country, Vásquez reveals that this is a land where Mexicans never lose their status as aliens. Near the end of the novel the author concentrates his attention on María Sandoval and her Anglo boyfriend, David Stiver. Her family accept David, but she is unable to enter his life except in a limited way. To his mother she is the "little Spanish girl," and David does not take her to his college fraternity parties. He desperately tries to invent for her an illustrious Spanish heritage so she will be "acceptable." When she gets pregnant, he forces her to have an abortion and she dies of complications. Vásquez inserts an ironic twist at the book's end, as David discovers that the family really *was* of the Spanish aristocracy and had at one time owned the land surrounding present-day Los Angeles.

Like *Pocho, Chicano* has been criticized for lacking focus and for a poor presentation of Chicano social realities. Frequently commentators liken it to a television soap opera, fraught with clichés and stereotypical characters, both Anglo and Chicano. Some critics feel it suffers from sketchy plot development; others condemn it for its bland and uninteresting style. Francisco Lomelí and Donaldo Urioste correctly define *Chicano*'s lasting role in the history of Mexican-American prose fiction to date. They contend that it "represented a daring attempt in 1970 to portray a Chicano theme, but has since been superseded by better novels."[5] It, like *Pocho*, is a seminal work, but suffers now from being too much a product of another time.

Vásquez's second novel was *Giant Killer*, issued in 1978. The protagonist here is Ramón García, a tough, big-city newspaper reporter who must save Los Angeles from the effects of race riots. Ron Singleton is the Anglo politician and Bucky Thompson the leader of a secret black faction. The author tries to make García a Chicano hero, but the result, in spite of a positive image of ethnic pride and racial harmony, is less than successful. *Another Land* (1982) concerns itself with Mexicans who enter and work illegally in the United States. While suspenseful and full of action, this novel has met with mixed critical attention, with adverse comments concerning its careless style and dull characterization.

NOVEL

A third novelist from the early period is Raymond Barrio, whose self-published work, *The Plum Plum Pickers*, a stylistic tour de force, remains a landmark novel of the social protest era. It appeared in 1969, and thus coincided with the activities of and corresponding media attention to labor leader César Chávez and his fledgling United Farmworkers Union. *The Plum Plum Pickers* develops in the imaginary community of Drawbridge, in California's Santa Clara Valley. Here the Chicano field workers live in miserable huts, pay too much for goods in the company store, work grueling and long hours, yet receive scarcely enough money to keep themselves fed a subsistence diet. The novel takes place in the months from May to December (the harvest months) and presents the life of a Mexican-American couple, Manuel and Lupe Gutiérrez, and their family. The Anglo villains are Morton J. Quill and Frederick C. Turner, foreman and owner respectively of the Western Grande Migrant Compound. Principally through interior monologue, Barrio reveals the thoughts and feelings of these characters and many more, while Anglo exploitation and greed flourish, and Chicano hopes and dreams are crushed by killing labor.

The technique of *The Plum Plum Pickers* reflects its theme; the reader must perform a Herculean labor to struggle through a maze of extraliterary material—radio broadcasts, graffiti, sketches, newspaper articles, and even Department of Agriculture instructions for the correct way to pick tomatoes. The result is marvelous. There is alliteration (as in the title) which reflects the drudgery of picking crops and some beautiful, highly poetic passages with descriptions of the gorgeous mountains and skies of the Monterey peninsula.

Most of the critical reception has been favorable, with quite accurate comparisons drawn to Upton Sinclair's *The Jungle* (1906), a novel documenting conditions among workers in the American meat-packing industry. *The Plum Plum Pickers* is an excellent exposure of the social and economic situation of the Chicano and Mexican migrant workers in the late 1960s, and its style did much to set the stage for future efforts by Chicano novelists.

The Most Influential Novelists

The novelists who began publishing between 1971 and 1975 are usually considered to be the most important, authors whose works have received the largest amount of critical acclaim both within the Chicano community and from non-Chicanos. They are Rudolfo Anaya, Ron Arias, Rolando Hinojosa-Smith, Miguel Méndez M., Alejandro Morales, and Tomás Rivera. All except Rivera are still alive and continue to add to the growing body of excellent Chicano fiction.

Rudolfo Anaya, professor of English at the University of New Mexico, published in 1972 what may be the largest-selling Chicano novel to date. *Bless Me, Última*, winner of the second annual Premio Quinto Sol National Literary Award, is set in a small northeastern New Mexico town in the 1940s and is concerned with the maturation of a young boy, Antonio Márez, and his relationship with his spiritual guide, the Última of the title. She is a *curandera*, a wise woman, a dispenser of curing herbs and potions who also heals with spiritual advice and some "magic." She is present from the boy's earliest experiences of growing up—family conflict, school, religion, evil, and death. The novel is narrated in the first person by Antonio, but the perspective is from a later time, when the narrator is older and more experienced. It takes place in the span of one year, during which Antonio loses his faith in traditional religion but enters into a new, more profound spiritualism. He also witnesses four deaths; the first three are terrifying and cause him to question religion and his place on earth; the last, Última's, leaves him soothed and confident.

There is much good in this novel: the beauty and magic of a wonderful New Mexico landscape, the legend of the Golden Carp (a god who becomes a fish in order to help his doomed people), and dream sequences as presentations of other dimensions of reality or as a means of foretelling the future. Anaya is adept at incorporating the rich folklore of his region, an element that is particularly important in the development of Chicano literature. As Raymund Paredes suggests, Anaya virtually immerses his protagonist in oral tradition, "by way of suggesting that for the Chicano, folklore is the foundation of a cultural identity."[6] *Bless Me, Última* is also concerned with time, since before the *curandera's* arrival Antonio lives in a magical childhood world.

Anaya's subsequent novels have not fared as well critically as his first, but this is perhaps because of the excellence of *Bless Me, Última,* and not so much because his other works are not sound. His second work, *Heart of Aztlán* (1976), is the story of Clemente and Adelita Chávez, who move to Albuquerque from the rural community of Guadalupe, a move they must make out of fiscal necessity. They settle in the downtown *barrio* of Barelas, where life is in stark contrast to their previous quiet and bountiful rural existence. The family members respond to an alien, urban environment: Clemente resorts to drink while the eldest son manages to adapt rather well; Benjie, the youngest, becomes an urban delinquent, a drug user, and perishes at the novel's end; the daughters cease attending school and rapidly lose their Chicana identity. The second son, Jasón (who also appeared in *Bless Me, Última*), yearns for his lost land as his father does, but nonetheless bears up to assume joint family leadership with his mother, whose stability and devotion to her family leave her virtually unaffected by the changes. A central figure is a blind poet, Crispín, a person much like Última. Crispín is the owner of a magical blue guitar. It is he who forces Clemente to assume responsibility for leading his people.

With its grim portrayal of the disastrous results of rural Chicano migration to the big city, *Heart of Aztlán* is frequently classified as a work of social protest. The problem with the novel, according to many critics, is

NOVEL

not so much a question of theme as one of craftsman-
ship. Bruce-Novoa, for instance, praises Anaya for exploring another literary space—the city—but calls *Heart*
less polished, less accomplished than his first novel.[7]

Tortuga (Turtle, 1979) has fared better with the critics. The title refers to the protagonist, a sixteen-year-old
paralyzed boy, so named because his body is encased in
a hard, shell-like cast. The novel is a first-person narrative of his long recovery from a near-fatal accident. During the course of his hospital journey from illness to
good health, Tortuga encounters many other crippled
children and an Última-like figure, Salomón, a mute
who communicates with the boy through a telepathy
process. Salomón introduces him to Tortuga Mountain,
a magical place which supplies the *agua bendita* (holy
water) from mineral springs that attract many sick people seeking miraculous cures. Tortuga also falls in love
with Ismelda, a nurse's aide, and after he leaves the
hospital he promises himself to return for her. *Tortuga* is
a novel rich with poetry, symbolism, dreams, and magical, mysterious characters.

Anaya's other works include a short story collec-
tion, *The Silence of the Llano* (1982); a short novel, *The
Legend of La Llorona* (1984), based on a famous figure of
Chicano and Mexican folklore; and *The Adventures of
Juan Chicaspatas* (1985), a mock-epic poem of the Chi-
cano political movement.

Ron Arias published a short novel in 1975, *The Road
to Tamazunchale*, which was nominated for the National
Book Award. It has been praised for bringing "contem-

porary Chicano fiction into an association with international literature and the arts that it has never before enjoyed."[8] It is the story of Don Fausto Tejada, an old, indigent Chicano who is dying. Instead of rolling over and accepting his death, the protagonist embarks on a mystical, magical, dreamlike journey with his niece and nurse, Carmen, and Marcelino, a flute-playing Peruvian shepherd. Occasionally joining them is Jesús, an urban Chicano whose sole occupation is hanging around the East Los Angeles streets. The old man takes control over his death, making the novel into a celebration of life, a rollicking journey culminating when Fausto joins his dead wife, Evangelina, at the close of the work. That is, it can be assumed that he joins his wife, because Arias blends reality and imagination, shifts his focus, and presents stories within stories so that the reader emerges from *Tamazunchale* with more questions than answers concerning death and reality. But it is comforting to witness the old man's journey as he vigorously attacks the death that awaits everyone.

Like many other Chicano novelists of the 1960s and 1970s, Arias presents much realistic detail from contemporary Chicano life. There is social commentary, especially concerning illegal Mexican workers, but, as Charles Tatum points out, Arias "is much too subtle a novelist blatantly to shout social messages," which are "implicit in the novel, veiled as they are in its magical realism."[9] It is this magical realism which has led quite a few scholars to compare *The Road to Tamazunchale* with modern Latin American novels such as Colombian Gabriel García Márquez's *One Hundred Years of Solitude* and Mexican Carlos Fuentes's *The Death of Artemio Cruz*. It has also been compared to the eighteenth-century British work by Laurence Sterne, *Tristram Shandy*, and to that masterpiece of Spanish literature of fantasy and reality, *Don Quijote de la Mancha* by Miguel de Cervantes. Lomelí and Urioste called it a "giant step in Chicano narrative,"[10] and José Armas wrote in the introduction to the second edition that this work is of "such magnitude that it will spark a new wave of experimentation in Chicano literature—a new level of consciousness not only of the essence of Chicanismo but also with the dimension of artistic expression which is at once distinctive and universal."[11] For all the praise it has received, however, *The Road to Tamazunchale* has occasionally been controversial in some circles because it is not principally a work of social or political realism.

Rolando Hinojosa-Smith is the most prolific Chicano novelist, with a half-dozen novels and a long list of periodical publications, ranging from short stories to entries for a Mexican-American devil's dictionary patterned after Ambrose Bierce's *Devil's Dictionary*. As a successful teacher and scholar, Hinojosa has also written frequently about Chicano literature. A Texan, Hinojosa grew up in the lower Rio Grande Valley, a place which serves as a setting for much of his work. He was twice in the army, the second time during the Korean conflict, an experience which later produced a collection entitled *Korean Love Songs: From Klail City Death Trip* (1978). He has MA and PhD degrees in Spanish literature and is currently professor of English at the University of Texas in Austin.

His first novel (which sometimes has been classified as a collection of short stories), *Estampas del Valle y Otras Obras/Sketches of the Valley and Other Works*, is a bilingual book with English translations by Gustavo Valadez. It was issued in 1973 and won the third annual Premio Quinto Sol prize. It is divided into four parts, each with a separate title: "Estampas del Valle" (Sketches of the Valley); "Por esas cosas que pasan" (For Those Things Which Happen); "Vidas y milagros" (Lives and Miracles); and "Una vida de Rafael Buenrostro (A Life of Rafael Buenrostro). The pieces take place in Belken County, Hinojosa's fictional south Texas community, during a time from the 1930s to the 1950s. There is an introductory note from the author/narrator with a warning that he will not explain anything and that he may not be relied upon to judge the reality or lack of it presented in the sketches. Jehú Malacara and Rafa Buenrostro also serve as narrators, so the reader receives several perspectives on the people and events in the region. There is a mosaic of the valley as the many characters appear and reappear in the short episodes, their lives intertwining. Hinojosa keeps the reader guessing as he supplies bits and pieces of information that are not understood until the book is finished; there is no linear time, and even places are only hazily identified.

Tatum correctly observes that the author intends to present, instead of a traditional mimetic novel with a

NOVEL

linear plot line, a prose tapestry of "the traditions and values that his Spanish-speaking community has shared for many generations and at least for as long as any of the characters can remember."[12] In the introduction to the first edition Herminio Ríos C. characterizes the importance of *Estampas* to Chicanos: it reveals "in a wide panoramic view, the vital strength of a people; one feels the heartbeat of a dynamic people; one feels life, love and hope."[13] Hinojosa, like many Chicano authors, presents contrasts and conflicts between Anglo and Chicano people, but he does so through irony, gentleness, and humor; the result is no less critical than is the work of his peers, and by no means less memorable.

In 1976 Hinojosa won acclaim outside the United States when *Klail City y sus alrededores* (Klail City and Its Surroundings) was published in Cuba and received the Premio Casa de Las Américas, a prestigious international award. The Spanish-language edition was thus distributed throughout the Hispanic world. The following year the book appeared in English with a Spanish title, *Generaciones y semblanzas* (Generations and Portraits), translated by Chicana poet Rosaura Sánchez. The style of *Klail City/Generaciones* continues in the same vein Hinojosa established in his first novel: fragmented time and space, shifting narration, and a phantasmagoria of characters.

Rafa Buenrostro and Jehú Malacara appear again, along with other figures such as Choche Markham, an Anglo politician, and Esteban Echeverría, an old man with a prodigious memory. There is a description of a fishing trip in Korea and an account of the death of Ambrosia Mora, a war veteran killed by an Anglo deputy sheriff who went unpunished for the crime. But no one person or story dominates; Klail City, its people, and its history/memory are the author's subjects. All of Hinojosa's writing forms one huge novel called *Klail City Death Trip*. With every appearance of each character, and with each tale told or retold from the memory of one or more characters, there are new images of and insights into both Chicano and Anglo life in the Rio Grande Valley.

Korean Love Songs: From Klail City Death Trip is a 53-page poetic interlude in Hinojosa's grand novel, a verse narration of Rafa Buenrostro's life during the Korean conflict. It is noteworthy that this entire book is in English (Hinojosa has remarked that the experience of the war was lived in English and he could write about it in no other way) and that the subtitle indicates the author's intention for it to be included with his prose as a part of the history of his community. Hinojosa calls it a novel in verse.

Hinojosa's next book was *Mi querido Rafa*, which was issued in 1981 and recast into English as *Dear Rafe* in 1985. The Spanish version received the Southwestern Conference on Latin American Studies Award in 1982. It is a two-part work, with the first twenty-three "chapters" consisting of letters from Jehú Malacara to Rafa Buenrostro. Part 2, "Soundings and Findings," is the work of the "writer," one P. Galindo. An introductory note proclaims that this section is added because Ga-

NOVEL

lindo "is convinced that not all bases are sufficiently covered" in the first section; thus, "he intends to add a shadow of his own once in a while, but always on the side of truth, that necessary element" (7). In the epistolary first part Jehú is employed at the Klail City Savings and Loan, where he works for an Anglo, Noddy Perkins. Jehú's letters reveal his growing discomfort with his job and with the Anglo families who control the Valley finances. At the close of the first section he mysteriously leaves town and heads off to Austin to attend the state university. P. Galindo sets out to discover why Jehú left; the second half of *Dear Rafe* consists of interviews with valley residents who give their accounts and perceptions of the people and events described in the letters. The story turns out to be a juicy one, with Jehú involved with several women, including Perkins's wife and Becky Escobar, a Chicano politician's wife. The picture of Jehú Malacara that emerges from all of this is neither bad nor good, and the reader is left to form his own opinions, not only of the characters, but also of the political and social situations prevailing in Klail City and its surroundings.

Hinojosa's next work, *Rites and Witnesses* (1982), carries the subtitle "A Comedy." Once again it is in the author's intriguing style: conversations, stories, documents, and commentary. This short work is also divided into two parts ("The Rites" and "The Witnesses") with a combined total of fifty-one vignettes. The time of the events is prior to those in *Dear Rafe*, but the characters again are Jehú and Rafa. The former has just begun to work at the bank, the first Chicano to do so, and the latter has just been wounded in Korea and transported home. Because this novel deals with the war and depicts two Chicanos in their first daily encounters with the Anglo world, it was originally written in English.

Partners in Crime: A Rafe Buenrostro Mystery (1985) is the next episode in *The Klail City Death Trip* series, but represents a departure from the style and tone of the other segments; in most respects this novel follows the conventional pattern and motifs of popular murder mysteries. Among the characters again is Rafe Buenrostro, a law school graduate who is now a lieutenant of the Belken County homicide squad. Jehú, back from graduate school, is cashier and vice-president of Klail City First National Bank. Belken County has been invaded by multinational corporations and crime on a large scale. The complexity of the events surrounding the three murders Rafe is investigating reveals Hinojosa's concern with truth, falsity, and meaning of events, both in fiction and in life.

Claros varones de Belken (Fair Gentlemen of Belken County), published in 1986, is yet another book featuring Rafa, Jehú, P. Galindo, and Esteban Echeverría. After finishing college Rafa goes off to Korea and returns at war's end. Jehú also serves in the army, but has become a missionary. Echeverría is the only person left in the Valley who remembers how it used to be. He "is the oldest of the old people who has seen all the revolutionaries buried. . . . This means that he is the last of the nineteenth-century litter that spent its whole life in the

Valley" (130). As the old man dies at the book's end, he reflects on the people he has known, the events he has witnessed, and the changes that have taken place.

Rolando Hinojosa-Smith must be recognized as a strong, innovative Chicano voice. His literary world of Klail City/Belken County, populated by scores of characters, both Anglo and Chicano, is a fascinating one. His style reflects the manner in which people perceive the ordinary, everyday world. The reader of Hinojosa's *Klail City Death Trip* series in effect becomes a citizen of the Rio Grande Valley and a participant in the life there. The writer's gentleness, kindness, and humor, his sometimes sarcastic and ironic style, combined with his multifaceted, complex characters, bring his world to life in all its shades and variety.

In 1974 a writer from Arizona published a novel which has become a classic for its use of language. *Peregrinos de Aztlán* (Pilgrims of Aztlán), by Miguel Méndez M., is set in the Mexican border town of Tijuana, and much of the stream-of-consciousness narration is Loreto Maldonado's memory fragments. Time is not linear; there is a juxtaposition of past and present. The dreams, dialogue, and multiple perspectives of a single episode demand an active reader for a full appreciation of this work. Linguistic sophistication is also required, as Méndez mixes standard Spanish, Mexican idiomatic and slang expressions, and a lot of *caló*, the street language used by many urban Chicanos.

Loreto Maldonado is an old man who once rode proudly with Pancho Villa during the 1910 revolution, but now is reduced to wandering the streets of Tijuana, washing tourists' cars. As he roams, people are presented through his eyes—Anglos, Chicanos, Mexicans, good folk and bad, millionaires, beggars, judges, and prostitutes. Some characters tell their stories in their own words. Loreto traces his roots to the Yaqui Indians of northern Mexico, and these roots provide a tie to the concept of Aztlán as a Chicano homeland. Méndez portrays the impact of city life on Chicanos as did Anaya in *Heart of Aztlán*, with a similar devastating result. The overall picture is of the myriad of poor and oppressed peoples who live along the 2000-mile-long border region between the United States and Mexico.

Peregrinos de Aztlán impresses with its presentation of themes and narrative style, but it is the author's use of language that sets it apart from other novels. As Marvin Lewis has pointed out,

The effective utilization of combinations of popular Spanish, official Spanish, and English to convey attitudes, situations, and images of reality contributes greatly to the novel's uniqueness as Chicano literature. Under the oppressive social conditions revealed in *Peregrinos de Aztlán*, language stands out as one of the most important vestiges of culture. Having one's own language in this case represents escape from a world that is insensitive and without understanding. The withdrawal is to a separate reality where new linguistic forms and meanings are created. Chicano language patterns remain a positive device with which to sustain the cultural struggle.[14]

NOVEL

Language serves another important purpose in that it links the modern Chicano novel with the oral literary tradition. The narration is not a sterile, impersonal voice; it is a common voice, one familiar to all. Méndez's second novel, *El Sueño de Santa María de las Piedras* (The Dream of Santa María de las Piedras), was published in Mexico in 1986. He has also written poetry and short stories, and is especially well known for the latter.

Alejandro Morales's first two novels, both written in Spanish, were published in Mexico City. *Caras viejas y vino nuevo* (Old Faces and New Wine, 1975), is dedicated to "mi barrio, que estará conmigo siempre" (my *barrio*, which will be with me always) and carries a note that the author hopes the day will come when he will not have to leave his native country to publish a novel in Spanish. It is the *barrio*, the Chicano section of a city, that Morales describes here, and it is more than a physical location; it is also a state of mind, a memory, a place where a Chicano can feel comfortable. Events are presented through the eyes of two teen-agers, Mateo and Julián. The episodes depicted occur in the 1950s and 1960s as the boys mature. Mateo is from a family that is sound, both emotionally and financially, and he expresses concern for those inhabitants of the *barrio* who are not as fortunate. Julián is completely different in that he has suffered much abuse from his father and consequently resorts to the use of drugs. After his mother dies, Julián and his father quarrel even more, until eventually the boy is killed in a car accident. Mateo observes the disintegration of the other youth's family, and this, combined with his other observations of *barrio* life, form Morales's novel. It ends on a poignant note as Mateo, a Chicano who had great promise, dies of leukemia.

There are other characters, Anglo and Chicano, and Morales does present positive aspects of *barrio* life to offset the negative ones. The language is realistic and graphic, so much so that some critics have called it pornographic. Overall, the novel attempts to interpret what Marvin Lewis has called the "internal functions" of the *barrio*.

Stylistically this book is a series of fragments, an attempt, according to one critic, "to approach reality through a manipulation of the novel's form," as the author "obscures the presence of a consistently discernible narrator," infuses "dialogue into narrative or descriptive text," and ignores "the mechanics of structure."[15] Like so many Chicano novels, *Caras* criticizes U.S. social fragmentation, but the criticism is filtered through the thoughts of a likable and sensitive young man. The English translation, done by short story writer Max Martínez and published in 1981 with editing and revisions by José Monleón and Alurista, has been a source of problems and concern because it is structured differently from the original.

La verdad sin voz (Truth without a Voice) of 1979 is a three-part work, in some respects a continuation of Morales's first novel, but different in others. In *La verdad* a character from *Caras*, Dr. Nagol, becomes Dr. Michael Logan (Nagol spelled backward), an Anglo. The story is set in a Texas town called Mathis, where Logan becomes director of the medical clinic. Much of the book is concerned with Logan's treatment of his Chicano patients as his marriage begins to fall apart. In the end Logan the idealist is killed by *Pistola gorda* (Fat Pistol), an Anglo policeman whose intimidation tactics allow him to rule the *barrio*. There are other major characters, among them Professor Morenito, who struggles to earn tenure at his university and, it is revealed at the novel's end, is the author of *La verdad sin voz*. Some of the people are Mexicans: El Señor Presidente—an unnamed Mexican president—and Casimiro, a revolutionary figure, for example. Through them and others the author portrays much of the Mexican social and political scene of the mid-1970s. Most of all, however, *La verdad* is concerned "with the negative economic impact of the United States upon Chicano culture and life's chances."[16]

The structure of this novel is somewhat different from that of *Caras*, in that there are three separate story lines (Logan, U.S.–Mexican government activities, and Professor Morenito) with alternating points of view. Stylistically Morales makes use of film techniques, and, as before, his language is frequently graphic. Erlinda Gonzales-Berry has called *La verdad sin voz* "one of the most sophisticated Chicano novels written to date," because it

demonstrates the writer's keen awareness of his craft. Most important of all, without abandoning his concern for the plight of his people, Morales moves away from the epic representation of Chicano reality and enters the true literary space of fiction: the portrayal of fully developed characters in contact with their environment and in search of truth.[17]

Morales's latest work is *Reto en el paraíso* (Reto in Paradise), published in the United States by Bilingual Press/Editorial Bilingüe in 1983. Its scope is broad, for it presents a history of a Spanish-Mexican land grant in California from approximately 1848 to the present. It is divided into eight chapters called *configuraciones* (configurations), each of which is made up of between eight and about fifty shorter divisions. Time alternates between present and past. One critic has said that *Reto* "sounds its message on many levels, in many voices and reveals worlds of Chicano heritage. With each reading we get a varied picture, a new kaleidoscopic view of the scene and the story line."[18] Other critics have compared the novel to Gabriel García Márquez's *One Hundred Years of Solitude*, a stylistically similar fictional treatment of the history of Colombia.

There are many characters in *Reto*, but a few emerge clearly enough to be called "principal." One of these is a Chicano, Dennis Berreyesa Coronel, an architect who has rejected his heritage. He struggles with his middle-class values and searches for his true identity, never really coming to terms with himself as the novel ends. Morales includes a long history of California from an Anglo viewpoint, following the James Lofford family through the patriarch's career beginning in the San Francisco gold rush of 1849 to the present, when his heir is Dennis's boss.

The style of this novel is complex; the reader is given bits and pieces which must be combined to form a broad view of the author's world, much as someone might put together a jigsaw puzzle. There is a combination of fantasy with elements of modern psychology. The book is truly bilingual in that large portions of the narration are in Spanish and equally large portions in English. It also is a work of metafiction, that is, self-conscious or self-referential. This is Morales's finest work; the characters are fascinating, the historical viewpoint varied and interesting, and the style and technique unforgettable. Victor Batiste was moved to call *Reto* "the first great novel of Chicano literature."[19] While this judgment may be a bit too enthusiastic, it is fair to call *Reto* one of the finest Chicano prose creations to date.

Tomás Rivera (1935–1984) was a much-respected poet, prose writer, scholar, and educator. A Texan, he held a BS in education, MED in educational administration, and MA and PhD in Romance languages and literatures. In 1979 he became chancellor of the University of California, Riverside, the first member of a minority ever to hold such a post in the entire history of the University of California system. In 1985 the Tomás Rivera Institute was established in Claremont, California, with 1.3 million dollars from the Carnegie Corporation of New York and the Los Angeles Times-Mirror Foundation.

Rivera left a significant body of work, both scholarly and creative, but his fame rests principally on a single collection of vignettes, sometimes classified as short stories, sometimes termed a novel. " . . . *y no se lo tragó la tierra"/And the Earth Did Not Part* first appeared in 1971 in a bilingual edition, with English translation by Herminio Ríos, and it has the distinction of being the first recipient of the Quinto Sol Award. It is a collection of fourteen pieces (some break it down as twelve—one for each month of the year—and opening and closing sections) and thirteen anecdotes which reflect the story preceding or serve as a preface for the next. The structural unity is provided by an unnamed Chicano migrant child who functions as a main character. In some of the episodes the narrative consists of the child's thoughts, impressions, and memories, while in others the thoughts come from other people. There are snatches of dialogue, prayers, and descriptive passages which form a picture of the "conflicts, both personal and collective, that the Chicano experiences within a socioeconomic environment that is hostile toward him in not offering equality on any terms. It is also the effort of people striving to define themselves."[20]

The work begins with a selection entitled "El año perdido" (The Lost Year), and that is precisely what the novel is, an account of incidents during the course of a year. The first paragraph sets the tone for the collection and provides an example of Rivera's style, which has been compared to that of Mexican novelist Juan Rulfo:

That year was lost to him. Sometimes he tried to remember but then when things appeared to be somewhat clear his thoughts would elude him. It usually began with a dream in which suddenly he thought he was awake, and then he would realize that he was actually asleep. That was why he could not be sure whether or not what he had recalled was actually what had happened.

One of the most memorable sections is "Cuando lleguemos" (When We Arrive), a series of internal monologues which are individual accounts of reactions to a twenty-four-hour truck ride. The story is a view of individuals trapped in a way of life that is always future oriented, aimed at some long-delayed arrival at the next field of crops. The title segment illustrates an aspect of this book which some critics contend to be its main focus—the maturation process of youth. The boy protagonist, angry at so much sickness and misfortune in his family, rebels against his faith: "Come now, do you really believe that? God, I am sure, doesn't give a damn about us" (51). Sure enough, the earth did not part and swallow him up for his doubts, as he had been told and believed.

The language of *Earth* is simple, uncomplicated, as are the thoughts of the people. This simplicity of language combines with the interior monologue form to produce a cinematic effect on a reader much like a stark, black-and-white movie might produce on a viewer. The structure is not so simple, as the reader must piece together and focus on the vignettes to sustain the structure. The combination of language and structure provides an everlasting image of the people and their travails. It is an excellent book which goes far beyond a simple description of the problems of Chicano life. "... *y no se lo tragó la tierra*" has received a great amount of critical attention, almost all favorable, and has been analyzed from many different perspectives. Joseph Sommers discusses the difficulties of critical discussion of the text; it

challenges the critical reader to analyze its formal characteristics and thus to decipher the cultural and historical meanings which lie beneath its surface. The work stands as a major contribution to Chicano narrative. . . . Only a multi-leveled and totalizing critical approach, capable of addressing itself to both the text and context, to form, meaning and values . . . can do it the critical justice it deserves.[21]

In 1987 novelist Rolando Hinojosa, a long-time friend of Tomás Rivera, recast the novel into English under the title *This Migrant Earth*.

Other Writers

Besides the preceding writers, who are the most influential and the most frequently named as "the best" Chicano novelists, there is a much larger group making contributions to the genre. This study will treat sixteen writers who have had considerable impact on the contemporary novel.

NOVEL

Aristeo Brito, born in the Mexican town of Ojinaga, across the border from Presidio, Texas, is another writer/professor who holds a PhD. His first work was *Cuentos i poemas de Aristeo Brito* (Stories and Poems by Aristeo Brito), which came out in 1974. His only novel to date is *El diablo en Texas* (The Devil in Texas), published in 1976 by Editorial Peregrinos, the same house that issued *Peregrinos de Aztlán*. Brito's novel is a short, three-part work with an introduction and an epilogue. Stylistically and thematically *Diablo*, like Tomás Rivera's novel, is frequently compared to Mexican writer Juan Rulfo's *Pedro Páramo* (1955). The three divisions in *Diablo* represent certain years in the history of the town of Presidio—1883, 1942, and 1970—and chronicle the spiritual disintegration of Chicano life because of Anglo influence. The reader must piece events together, for the author does not tell his tale in a straightforward manner. The first section is about Anglo settlers who take over Mexican lands in Texas and the subsequent Mexican-American resistance. The second part takes place during World War II and presents zoot-suit-clad Chicanos and a high level of racial tension. Most of the once-proud Mexican landowners in the area are reduced to working as pickers in fields. In the 1970 section a prominent character returns to his hometown to attend his father's funeral and decides to remain and work for change in the lives of his people and an improvement of their circumstances.

Important aspects of *Diablo* are its characters and its language, which has been compared to that found in

Peregrinos de Aztlán. Some critics have not taken too kindly to the book for various reasons: lack of unity, too much similarity to previous Chicano novels with no further development, and failure to portray the Anglo as a demonic figure—the devil of the title. Others praise *Diablo* for the author's use of folk-based fantasy as a means of transforming history into myth and for his careful attention to historical and linguistic details.

Nash Candelaria has made a significant contribution to the Mexican-American historical novel with his trilogy of New Mexico. In *Memories of the Alhambra* (1977) the protagonist leaves his family in search of his ancestral past, a past he hopes to find in Spain. José Rafa is looking for genealogical validation of a life marred by ethnic prejudice. His search leads him first to Mexico, where he is initially comforted by seeing many other brown-skinned people, but he singlemindedly continues on his journey to Spain, where he desperately desires to discover that he is Spanish. The reader necessarily finds José's denial of his own racial identity troubling, but it is set within a series of dreams and flashbacks that illuminate his past and reveal his fears. The protagonist expects to overcome his pain of rejection by denying his identity and finding one that is socially acceptable.

José's son, Joe, grows up in California but makes summer trips to New Mexico. The younger Rafa has been assimilated into Anglo culture; he has a college education and marries an Anglo. Joe's thoughts on his father's crisis add an interesting perspective to this novel, for, as Joe expresses it, his father has earned for his son the right to succeed, and now Joe wants his children to have the right to fail and still be accepted. Certainly Candelaria's novel goes against the grain of most Chicano novels in its acceptance of assimilation, but it also features a tragic character whose denial of his identity is morally and culturally unacceptable.

In 1982 Candelaria published his second novel of the Rafa trilogy. *Not by the Sword* focuses on the years of the Mexican-American War, 1846–1848. The theme of identity explored in depth in *Memories* here takes on secondary importance to the theme of heritage and tradition. The Rafa family finds itself about to become absorbed by the westward-moving Yankees. Conflict between Anglos and Mexicans, the fight of the latter to preserve their land, and the threat to traditional ways of life are the primary plot elements. José Rafa III, the younger son, has become a priest, according to family tradition, while his older brother and twin, Carlos, has been trained to manage the family land. But the historical moment determines otherwise, as Carlos becomes embroiled in the conflict with the Anglos and is killed. José leaves the priesthood in order to take his brother's place, marry, and continue the family name. Within this plot outline the teaching of the patriarch, José's grandfather, provides the framework within which the family functions; namely, that historical events are cyclical, that all of this has happened before, and finally that "the right people are Spanish and they own land" (110). The fact that the Spanish took the land from the Indians appears to mitigate the crimes the Anglos commit against the Mexican landowners, and suggests that change and adaptation are natural and necessary.

Inheritance of Strangers (1985) provides another link in the history of the Rafa family, covering a period some decades later in the life of José Rafa III. Family fortunes have declined, although José is still a respected member of the community. There are two plots, the "present" one dealing with the conflict and violence surrounding a local election, and the "past" one concerning Uncle Pedro, the mad member of the family who lives locked in a shed. The dual narratives reflect each other because both center on dispossession, the takeover by the Anglos, and the tenacity of the Hispanos in retaining dignity and pride in their heritage.

Again the theme of historical repetition is overtly present, but Candelaria's third book communicates the New Mexican past with a stronger sense of the importance of heritage and of oral tradition as a means of preserving it. José Rafa narrates the sad family history, focusing on the tragedy of Uncle Pedro, whose family lost everything in California. At the novel's end the grandson to whom the eldest Rafa is telling the story is killed; this death again threatens family continuity. The protagonist, however, takes up the story with the next grandson, beginning, "Once upon a time . . . there was a land called New Mexico."

Nash Candelaria's novels express the conflicts inherent in a society that is largely defined in terms of conquest. *Memories* takes a disturbing look at a "New" Mexican who wants to believe that he is Spanish, and the other two novels depict the resiliency of the culture in crisis of the first book. Candelaria's work proposes a notion of the oneness of humankind that is not typical of most Chicano literature, which usually proclaims the singularity of Chicano culture.

Celso A. de Casas is a Californian who published *Pelón Drops Out* in 1979. This book is a rollicking, self-conscious spoof of writings of the 60s-generation cult figure Carlos Castaneda, author of *The Teachings of Don Juan.* The first chapter of *Pelón*, "What it am?" by "author" Pelón Palomares, sets the tone for the work: "This book is meant to make people laugh, though here and there I slipped in some serious thoughts to show my philosophical talent." It ends with a poem in Spanish and English, with these final lines:

> To end this thing, let me just say,
> hope it brought laughter to your day.
> It was nice to write, lots of fun,
> but now I'm sad so the book is done.
> What, you wonder, is the matter with him?
> I can't hear you laughing and my spirit is dim.
> Have no care and don't let it bug you,
> it's only temporary, like the flu.
> Part of the reason is my mind is a tank,
> it fills with joy when there's money in the bank.

The story in between is about the protagonist's apprenticeship with two masons and the adventures they have together.

Lionel G. García is a practicing veterinarian who published his first novel, *Leaving Home*, in 1985. The story takes place in southern California in the late 1930s and the 1940s and is a picaresque tale. The protagonist is Adolfo Argüelles, a famous baseball pitcher who once played for the New York Yankees and the St. Louis Cardinals. He is an old man constantly in pursuit of women, partially for sexual fulfillment, partly for true love. García's second novel, *A Shroud in the Family* (1987), features a protagonist suffering an identity crisis (his psychiatrist has told him that he lacks an identity), and overwhelmed by the political and social problems of the Mexican-American. Set in Houston, the novel features a large group of characters, many of whom are members of a Chicano family whose history reveals the truth about the mythologized saga of Texas.

Below the Summit, by Joseph V. Torres-Metzgar (1976), is a curious Chicano novel in that the protagonist is a racist. Robby Lee Cross is a fundamentalist preacher, married, ironically, to a Chicana, Maria Dolores, whom he insists on calling Marie. The tone, language, and imagery of the book are biblical—it is set in Geneva Gap in west Texas, described as "God's Country" and "A Pisgah Sight." During the course of the narrative Robby Lee is time and again frustrated—sexually, spiritually, culturally, and emotionally—until he finally goes berserk and kills his wife. At the local college there is an evil Dr. Sterner, who preaches against "social irresponsibility, whiskey and niggers," and Dr. Serveto, a Chicano who dares to challenge the students' complacency about race and culture, for which he is ultimately burned in effigy. *Below the Sum-*

mit presents a perverted picture of an Anglo paradise in which anyone who does not conform to the rule of the majority is quickly sacrificed. It is a very unusual work, outside the general realm of Chicano literature, and it consequently has received minimal critical attention.

Macho! by Edmund Villaseñor sprang onto the scene in 1973 with a gaudy paperback cover proclaiming it "The First Great Chicano Novel." It is not the first, and it is far from great. It is about Roberto García, a seventeen-year-old Mexican Indian who spends about half the book getting out of Mexico, past the infamous ports of entry for *braceros*. Once in the United States, he sets out to prove his *machismo*, his masculine superiority, by working at a killing pace; he robs and cheats his fellow laborers, breaks strikes, and eventually makes a great deal of money. Most critics dislike *Macho!* for sound reasons: cardboard characterizations, lack of a political stance, and stiff language, especially in dialogue. Lomelí and Urioste condemn it as "one of the most opportunistic efforts to exploit a new [in 1973] taste for Chicano themes."[22] *Macho!* was reviewed throughout the country, thus making it a highly visible Chicano novel.

Nambé—Year One, by Orlando Romero (1976), is a very personal book, written in the form of an autobiography of Mateo Romero, who lives in the village of Nambé, New Mexico. It is a presentation of the narrator's thoughts, with continual shifts in time from childhood to adulthood to teen years, with no continuous pattern. Much of the novel's focus is on a gypsy woman who is the object of Mateo's affection. She eventually becomes a symbol of abandonment of tradition, since the narrator would be forced to leave his land, his home, and his family if he were to follow her. The book ends as he writes a farewell letter, stating, "I cannot bear it, but I must say goodbye . . . until, perhaps, my son or my grandson is afflicted by the same love."

Nambé—Year One can be compared to *Bless Me, Última* in its New Mexican rural setting, as well as its use of legends, folklore, dreams, and mysticism. It is also similar to Anaya's novel in that the protagonist must learn about himself, particularly his relationship with his history and environment. What little critical attention *Nambé* has received has generally been favorable. Joe Rodríguez places the book quite accurately in the development of the modern Chicano novel when he calls it "part of a trend . . . which conceives of a place, its history and its landscape as a protagonist, together with the human beings who figure as main characters in a narrative."[23] Romero also writes poetry and short fiction, and is a sculptor.

The Rain God: A Desert Tale (1984), a first novel by Arturo Islas, a professor at Stanford University, is the story of three generations of the Angel family of El Paso. It is a partially autobiographical novel, frequently focusing on the grandson, Miguel Chico, a writer. The book explores the Chicano's identification with his Mexican past (the Aztec rain god of the title) and is yet another view of life in the border region. Its original title, *Día de los muertos/Day of the Dead*, points to another theme, the Anglo versus Chicano views of death. Stylistically *The*

Rain God is rather complex in that it is divided into six "stories" with a single, omniscient narrator, but with discontinuous time, flashbacks, and interior monologues; there is also much symbolism. It is in the tradition of the modern Latin American novel of magic realism.

Muerte en una estrella (Death in a Star), by poet Sergio Elizondo, was published in Mexico in 1984. The novel is about two boys, young Texans born in the United States of Mexican parents, who enroll in a Job Corps program. There is little action in this collage of monologue, dialogue, and stream-of-consciousness narration. Sometimes there is a narrator, a balladeer who comments on the events, frequently addressing the reader as "you." Oscar and Valentín (age sixteen and nineteen—occasionally identified only by the numbers) go to a circus in Austin, steal a car, and are shot by the police. As the author sketches in his characters, the reader learns about their lives and their parents: migrant work, union strikes, poor living conditions, bleak future. The last chapter is really a short play, as the author describes the setting, sets the scene, identifies the actors, and describes the situation. It is a dialogue between the boys as they lie dying under the stars of the Lone Star state. *Muerte en una estrella* is a finely wrought work, combining social commentary with the relation of deep personal tragedy; stylistically it is a musical dance through time and space.

Two good novelists whose works are sometimes overlooked in Chicano literature are John Rechy and Floyd Salas. Their omission is perhaps due to the fact that they do not write specifically about experiences common to Chicanos. Rechy has emphasized homosexual themes, while Salas treats prison experiences or life in the San Francisco Bay area in the turbulent 1960s.

Rechy's books include *City of Night* (1963) and *This Day's Death* (1969). The protagonist in the former leaves his native city of El Paso and travels the country in search of his identity. He goes to the major cities—New York, Chicago, New Orleans, San Francisco, Los Angeles—and experiences the dark side of homosexual life in urban America. In the latter work the principal character is again from El Paso; Jim Girard is a Chicano who tries to escape from his hypochondriac mother by fleeing to Los Angeles, where he experiences discrimination in the courts because of his homosexuality. John Chávez has written about Rechy's work and concludes that he

has occasionally written sketches on Chicano topics, and his ethnicity has in one way or another influenced all of his books. Whether Chicano literature is defined as literary work produced about Mexican-Americans or by them, his works can be included in that category, especially since their plots usually contain some Mexican details and their themes frequently derive, at least in part, from Chicano culture. Indeed, the major theme of Rechy's works, his characters' desperate search for communion with others, results as much from his Chicano childhood as from his homosexual lifestyle.[24]

NOVEL

John Rechy has written another half-dozen novels and several short essays; his sketch "El Paso del Norte" has been included in several Chicano anthologies.

Floyd Salas has published three novels. His first, *Tattoo the Wicked Cross* (1967), was characterized as one of the best "and most important first novels published in America during the past ten years."[25] The protagonist is a fifteen-year-old *pachuco* gang member, Aaron D'Aragon, who has been sent to jail for minor crimes. The book describes the brutal life in prison as the young man is forced to become a murderer in order to survive. *What Now My Love* (1970) is about a teacher who gets involved in the drug subculture of San Francisco in the late 1960s. Miles and his friends flee the country after a shooting which takes place during a drug raid. They settle in the Mexican border town of Tijuana for a time, but as the novel closes, Miles returns to the United States to accept his fate. *Lay My Body on the Line* (1978) is about another teacher, who is also a boxer and ex-prisoner. Roger Leon is a paranoid who survives a series of shattering experiences. Charles Tatum characterizes this book as Salas's most interesting work because he "effectively recreates the rapidly alternating excitement and depression of one of the most volatile periods in American history."[26]

It is only in the last decade or so that novels by women have been published. Several critics have remarked that the relative scarcity of female novelists is because Chicanas represent a minority within a minority. They have not produced the same quantity of long prose fiction as men for various reasons: social and historical factors, lack of support and encouragement from their families or others in their group, and reluctance of even Chicano publishing houses to print their work. Along with a lack of novels there has been a corresponding scarcity of critical studies of even those few novels in print.

The first Chicana novel is *Come Down from the Mound* (1975), by Berta Ornelas. The protagonist is Aurora Alba, a political and social activist. She is linked romantically with Jesús (Chuy) Santana, a city commissioner with an obsession for political power. The central theme is love versus power as Chuy wants to conquer Aurora physically, and also wishes to win her over politically. Francisco Lomelí is one of the few critics to survey the Chicana novel and finds fault with this one: shallow story line, a glossing over of ideological concerns, and the language, which he perceives as mocking Spanish speakers.[27] It is noteworthy, however, because it presents the feminine viewpoint for the first time.

In 1976 Isabella Ríos published *Victuum*, characterized as the earliest example in Chicano literature of a work dealing with psychic phenomena. Lomelí calls it the first *Bildungsroman* (novel of self-discovery) about a Chicana, and a "complete representation of a woman's psyche in its various stages of development within the metaphysical context of the universe."[28] The protagonist is Valentina Ballesternos, who serves as the first-person

NOVEL

narrator. Part 1 is her development to her mid-teens, while the shorter second section deals with about thirty years of her adult life. The entire story, her quest for knowledge, is developed as if it were seen through Valentina's eyes, so the reader receives only her thoughts and perceptions. Among her many mental encounters with real or mythological beings there is the title character, Victuum, a planetary prince of knowledge. The work is virtually without plot and devoid of action; it ends with a confused protagonist.

Gina Valdés, a Californian who spent her early years in Mexico, published a highly autobiographical novel, *María Portillo*, as the fourth and longest part of a 1981 collection of four interrelated stories entitled *There Are No Madmen Here*. The first work, "Rhythms," concentrates on María's daughter, Yoli, who daydreams along with her girlfriend in their history class. In "Nobody Listens" María's father, Don Severino, leads a lonely life in a run-down hotel. The third part is the title story, which centers on María's brother, Chuy, who is confined to an asylum. These first three stories set the stage for the fourth, which deals with an abandoned mother of three who must struggle to earn a living in Los Angeles. She receives support from her large extended family, on both sides of the Mexican border, and it is the strength of such a family that provides the novel's theme. The protagonist emerges from the novel independent, self-reliant, a true heroine who has prevailed in spite of harsh socioeconomic realities.

However, as she succeeds in forging a better life for her daughter, she must recognize and face the reality that their lives are radically changed, for better or worse, by their growing up in an Anglo environment.

Trini, by short story writer and dramatist Estela Portillo Trambley, is a 1986 novel which incorporates many of the same themes of her work in other genres. It is yet another story of self-discovery, this time of a Tarahumara Indian woman who leaves her native Mexico and illegally crosses the border into the United States, where she wishes to give birth to her child and to achieve a dream of owning land. The story is one of a quest for a different life, a journey to another world. There is a blending of Indian and Christian themes. At the book's end, her goals accomplished, she realizes she must return home to reestablish her ties with her native country and to introduce her children to the good and beautiful elements of her old life.

One of the most promising novelists is Ana Castillo, whose *The Mixquiahuala Letters* (1986) is an epistolary novel consisting of forty letters sent by Teresa, a poet, to her artist friend Alicia. At the beginning of the book Castillo informs the reader that the letters are not to be "read in the usual sequence. All letters are numbered to aid in following any one of the author's proposed options." She provides a reading order for three types of people—the conformist, the cynic, and the quixotic—and adds that each letter can also be read separately as a piece of short fiction. Castillo's dedicatory note quite appropriately pays homage to Julio Cortázar, the Argentine author of *Rayuela* (Hopscotch), a 1963 novel that provides the reader with two separate orders in which to read. Castillo takes Cortázar's strategy for creative reading a step further by forcing the reader to assume an identity and participate in the game with a "personality." None of the three approaches allows for a reading of all the letters: the conformist sees twenty-nine, the cynic thirty-two, and the quixotic thirty-four. Twenty-three "core" letters are read by all three, while only the quixotic reads the first chapter and the conformist the last. Each type reads either one or two letters out of the 1–40 numerical sequence in which they are printed.

The Mixquiahuala Letters chronicles the lives of two women from the United States, beginning with their first meeting in Mexico and continuing over the course of a decade to a tragic event in one woman's life. Since all the documents are products of Teresa's pen, the reader sees only her viewpoint and her interpretation of those written by Alicia. Many letters deal with their Mexican travels together and the events in their lives as they visit several large U.S. cities. This novel is about relationships: among women and between women and men. It is an innovative, compelling, and captivating book which reveals a great deal about male-female relationships, both in Mexico and in the United States, while it explores the modern woman's attempts to change her role and status in traditional, male-dominated societies.

Any summary commentary concerning the post–1959 Chicano novel must recognize the vitality of the genre along with the broad and varied treatments of themes. To date it remains the only literary form written by Chicanos to attract more than passing national attention from the U.S. literary establishment.

Notes

1. Nicolás Kanellos, "*Las aventuras de Don Chipote*, Obra precursora de la novela chicana," *Hispania* 67, 3 (Sept. 1984): 358–63.

2. Raymund A. Paredes, "The Evolution of Chicano Literature," *MELUS* 5, 5 (Summer 1978): 85–110.

3. Mario Suárez, "El Hoyo," *Arizona Quarterly* 3 (Summer 1947): 114–15.

4. "Cannery Worker Writes Novel about Mexican-Americans' Life," *San Jose Evening News* 28 Oct. 1959: 12.

5. Francisco A. Lomelí and Donaldo W. Urioste, *Chicano Perspectives in Literature: A Critical and Annotated Bibliography* (Albuquerque: Pajarito Publications, 1976) 49.

6. Paredes 102.

7. Bruce-Novoa, *Chicano Authors: Inquiry by Interview* (Austin: University of Texas Press, 1980) 184.

8. Eliud Martínez, "Ron Arias' *The Road to Tamazunchale:* A Chicano Novel of the New Reality," *Contemporary Chicano Fiction*, ed. Vernon E. Lattin (Binghamton, NY: Bilingual Press/Editorial Bilingüe, 1986) 226.

9. Charles M. Tatum, *Chicano Literature* (Boston: Twayne, 1982) 130.

10. Lomelí and Urioste 42.

11. José Armas, introduction, *The Road to Tamazunchale* by Ron Arias. (2d ed.; Albuquerque: Pajarito Publications 1978) 14.

12. Tatum 122.

13. Herminio Ríos C., introduction, *Estampas del valle y otras obras/*

NOVEL

Sketches of the Valley and Other Works by Rolando Hinojosa-Smith (Berkeley: Quinto Sol Publications, 1973) 9.

14. Marvin A. Lewis, *Introduction to the Chicano Novel* (Milwaukee: University of Wisconsin Spanish-Speaking Outreach Institute, 1982) 18.

15. John C. Akers, "Fragmentation in the Chicano Novel: Literary Technique and Cultural Identity" *International Studies in Honor of Tomás Rivera*, ed. Julián Olivares (Houston: Arte Público Press, 1986), 125.

16. Lewis 37.

17. Erlinda Gonzales-Berry, "Alejandro Morales," *Chicano Literature: A Reference Guide*, ed. Julio A. Martínez and Francisco A. Lomelí (Westport, CT: Greenwood Press, 1985) 307.

18. Víctor N. Batiste, review of "Reto en el paraiso," *Revista Chicano-Riqueña* 13, 1 (Spring 1985): 91.

19. Batiste 94.

20. Oscar Urquídez-Somoza, "Tomás Rivera," Martínez and Lomelí 342.

21. Joseph Sommers, "Interpreting Tomás Rivera," *Modern Chicano Writers*, ed. Joseph Sommers and Tomás Ybarra-Frausto (Englewood Cliffs, NJ: Prentice-Hall, 1979) 107.

22. Lomelí and Urioste 50.

23. Joe Rodríguez, "Orlando Romero," Martínez and Lomelí 350.

24. John Chávez, "John Francisco Rechy," Martínez and Lomelí 323.

25. C. Michael Curtis, "Bestiality Behind Bars," review of *Tattoo the Wicked Cross* by Floyd Salas, *Saturday Review* 23 Sept. 1967: 82.

26. Tatum, 136.

27. Francisco A. Lomelí, "Chicana Novelists in the Process of Creating Fictive Voices," *Beyond Stereotypes: The Critical Analysis of Chicana Literature*, ed. María Herrera-Sobek (Binghamton, NY: Bilingual Press/Editorial Bilingüe, 1985) 39.

28. Lomelí 40.

CHAPTER 4

The Short Story

The genre of the short story has been an extremely popular one with Mexican-American writers in recent years. It has lent itself to the often-felt desire to communicate significant moments in the lives of Chicano people, moments which, when accumulated, reveal the soul, heart, and mind of *La Raza.* Chicano short fiction treats a wide variety of themes, expressed in great multiplicity of styles, but many concerns of Chicano literature in general are clearly present: the question of identity, the concept of home (the *barrio,* the U.S.–Mexican border, Aztlán), relations with the Anglo, migrant life, the family, and the role of women, among others. In addition to the presentation of contemporary life Chicano writers frequently turn to traditional folk motifs, such as the ghost story and legendary or mythical figures. Fantasy and folklore have not been driven out by modern, urban topics. Chicano short stories are rich in their variety of themes and voices.

The following survey treats those authors who have

published complete collections, except for Mario Suárez, whose works will be discussed separately.

Mario Suárez

Mario Suárez has been called the first truly "Chicano" writer because he was comfortable with the name (many of his predecessors and contemporaries were not) and recognized the importance of the term as a symbol of pride. His most famous story, "El Hoyo," is a short narrative sketch with the Tucson *barrio* of the title as protagonist. It is an anecdotal portrayal of the inhabitants and their activities, told by a loving yet sometimes critical narrator. Another story, "Señor Garza," is a masterful character study of one of El Hoyo's barbers, a philosophical man whose profession brings him into contact with all sorts of people, from zoot suiters to politicians. He accommodates his language and topics of conversation to those of his clients. Suárez tells Garza's life story, from birth, through school and jobs, to his present situation. The barber's thoughts serve as a filter through which the author presents an honest, critical, yet gentle view of the people in the *barrio*.

"Maestría" is a lament for the "good old days"—in this case Mexican—when a man referred to as a *maestro* was a master of "whatever trade, art or folly he practices." Suárez couches his didactic commentary in the story of Gonzalo Pereda, a *maestro* who owns a small saddle shop but whose passion is cockfighting. His beloved Killer is a champion rooster who triumphs several times before being severely injured. During the bird's convalescence Gonzalo accidentally chokes it to death, giving the narrator occasion to warn of a dying culture. With his literary portraits of the old ways of life and the new, Mario Suárez is a pivotal figure in the history of Chicano literature.

Writers with Published Collections

While Mario Suárez described life among Chicanos in the city of Tucson, Arizona, Sabine Reyes Ulibarrí in his three collections of short stories presents a view of a small community high in the mountains of northern New Mexico. The majority of the people there are descendants of the first non-Indian colonists, and their principal language is Spanish, frequently peppered with obsolete sixteenth-century forms. Their religion is staunchly Catholic. Ulibarrí grew up in the county of Tierra Amarilla, the title of his first volume (1964), where the land and its people so impressed him that he committed his memories of them to paper.

"Mi caballo mago" (My Wonder Horse) illustrates the folkloric quality of many of Ulibarrí's stories. It is about a young boy's capture of a legendary white stallion who subsequently escapes. The lad is full of sorrow, but also joy because he comprehends the animal's indomitable spirit and need for freedom. "El relleno de Dios" (The Stuffing of the Lord) is a touching portrait of a village priest, an Anglo whose Spanish is energetic but not very accurate. He confuses "el *reino* de Dios," the kingdom of God, with *relleno*, which is the concoction traditionally placed in the cavity of a Thanksgiving turkey. It is a humorous tale of the great warmth and laughter a kindly priest brought into the lives of his parishioners; it illustrates the innocent and fun-loving aspects of the small community.

Ulibarrí's second collection, *Mi abuela fumaba puros/ My Grandma Smoked Cigars* (1977), continues in the same folkloric vein. The writer captures the collective imagination of his region in "¿Brujerías o tonterías? (Witcheries or Tomfooleries), an account of local witches, healers, and La Llorona, a legendary woman who walks the earth lamenting the death of her children. The author's straightforward, conversational style is exemplified by the story's closing paragraph: "Well, amigos, I could tell you more witcheries, but let's leave them for another time. But I want to tell you that what I have told you happened exactly as I have narrated it, as I saw and understood it in those years and in that place, Tierra Amarilla."

Primeros encuentros/First Encounters (1982), continues to evoke the imaginary past of the author's home, but there is a new and significant addition here: the encounters of the title are the inhabitants' first experiences with people of another, quite different culture. The first story, "El forastero gentil" (The Gallant Stranger), is about a *gringo* who appears one day at the narrator's home. Dan Kraven's horse has broken a leg, and Kraven is forced to shoot it. The narrator and his family are somewhat distrustful of the stranger, but take him in nonetheless. They grow fond of him during his week's stay, but he soon must leave, and requests a favorite horse which he is granted out of courtesy. Then, "he went into the sun and disappeared forever." As time passed, Kraven became the subject of family lore as they exchanged memories of him. One morning they found he had returned and left gifts for all, including a beautiful palomino horse to replace the borrowed one. The narrator closes the story with an address to the honorable stranger:

Our memories of you, my family's and also my own,
Dan Kraven, so that everyone may know. I want
everyone to know that long ago in a Hispanic place, in
a Spanish-speaking New Mexico, there was a gentle
gringo who was gracious and generous. My silent and
mysterious knight errant, don't say a word. I'll say it
for you (10).

Thus Sabine Ulibarrí completes (for now) his history of Tierra Amarilla with the entrance of the Anglo onto one family's land and his lasting influence. The author's portrait of the people and history of his region is an intimate, loving, and somewhat nostalgic one. He is a master at evoking the spirit and vitality of an ancient yet changing way of life.

   Cachito Mío (My Cachito), by José Acosta Torres, is a bilingual collection of fifteen exemplary tales, published in 1973. It is in the oral tradition of the fourteenth-

SHORT STORY

century Spanish writer Juan Manuel, whose *El Conde Lucanor* (Count Lucanor) is a series of anecdotes in which a young nobleman receives advice and wisdom from his counselor, Patronio, in the form of moral tales. In Torres's book Cachito learns from his father, a simple man. The stories' themes are bilingualism, death, war, music, and play.

Also published in 1973 is a collection of twelve stories and a play, *Blue Day on Main Street*, by J. L. Navarro. Although the setting for the pieces is both rural and urban, the focus is on the urban Chicano trying to survive in a world of drugs, prostitution, and violence. A variety of stylistic approaches is employed, including fantasy, interior monologue, and graphic realism. The title story, "Blue Day on Main Street," is told in the words of a man recently released from a mental hospital. As he stands on Main Street in downtown Los Angeles, he muses: "As I look around me, I can't help thinking that what I see is just an extension of the place I left behind" (65). The protagonist of "Eddie's Number" is a heroin addict who dies violently, while "Tamale Leopard" deals with prostitution.

Estela Portillo Trambley's book entitled *Rain of Scorpions and Other Writings* (1975) is a landmark in Chicano literature because she is the first major female prose writer to publish her work. In 1973 she was editor of an issue of *El Grito*, the first instance of a Chicano literary journal featuring work by women. There is a feminist strain in all of Portillo Trambley's work, prose fiction and drama alike. Like many Chicano writers she is critical not only of American society but also of some Chicano traditions and social structures.

The title story draws on the myths of paradise, the promised land, and the great flood, common to many mythologies, and provides an example of the author's many strong female characters. "Rain of Scorpions" takes place in a small mining town near El Paso, where a Vietnam war veteran, Fito, tries to organize the townspeople to resist social oppression and ecological destruction by the mine owners. As a consequence of his acts five boys set out to discover a new place to live, an apocryphal green valley. The town is devastated by a flood which unearths a huge nest of scorpions. The catastrophe brings Fito together with a woman called Lupe, and they, like Noah and his wife after the biblical flood, begin life anew. Lupe is a large woman who at one point claims to be Mother Earth; she, like many of Portillo Trambley's women characters, decides on her own role in life rather than having it dictated to her by men.

The title of Saul Sánchez's 1977 collection, *Hay Plesha Lichans tu di Flac* (I Pledge Allegiance to the Flag), prepares the reader for the cultural problems explored in many of the stories. In two "bookend" stories the saying of the pledge is central. In the first piece, "El primer día de la escuela" (The First Day of School), a Mexican-American child is punished for not being able to pronounce the words. In the final story, "The Funeral," the narrator notes that the Mexican-American parents of a dead soldier receive the flag from his grave

SHORT STORY

but do not know how to say the "Hay plesha lichans." The story poignantly suggests the ultimate sacrifice many Chicanos made to the Vietnam war, while not having a powerful enough voice with which to express their sacrifice. Many of the other stories deal with the problem of speaking English and the harsh lives of Chicano migrant workers.

Miguel Méndez's works, both in *Cuentos para niños traviesos* (Stories for Naughty Children, 1979) and *Tata Casehua y otros cuentos* (Tata Casehua and Other Stories, 1980), provide some of the best examples of stories that duplicate the long and important oral tradition in Chicano literature. His first collection contains some narrations that are the author's adaptations of old folktales from the Mexican border region. Others are patterned on tales from *Calila et Dimna* (1251), one of the earliest examples of prose fiction translated into the Spanish language. In the preface to *Niños*, Méndez states that his wish in basing his writing on ancient sources is that "what is ours may flow and become revitalized, so that our Chicano people may have the pride and the spiritual potential that their grand ancestral culture has reserved for them," because "what is inherited cannot be stolen. We, surely, are heirs of a vast culture."

"Doña Emetería" is a story reflecting the exacting life of the border region. The hundred-year-old woman of the title suffers from headaches when she does not get her coffee, an expensive commodity. A great-grandchild finds eggs that can be exchanged for coffee at the store, but on his return, he and his cousin are attacked by vicious youngsters who force them to drop the precious grounds, which disappear in the desert sands. The sketch ends with the title character waiting in front of her house, expecting to brew the coffee.

"Mother Roadrunner and the Serpent" is a folktale about a careless bird who leaves her newly hatched chicks alone, providing a serpent the opportunity to eat all save one. A flying squirrel tells her how to get even: she is to place some fish in front of the snake's den so that the lion, his mortal enemy, will kill him when he emerges. The lion does so, but in searching about for the fish finds and eats her remaining chick. This tale is a chilling example of a traditional children's fairy tale adapted to a southwestern setting.

Tata Casehua y otros cuentos is a bilingual collection of nine works, with translations by Eva Price. The title story, one of the most famous in Chicano literature, was originally published in the journal *El Grito* in 1968. Tata Casehua is an old Yaqui Indian who wanders through the great Sonoran Desert of northern Mexico and the southern United States. He seeks someone to whom he can leave his tribe's history and traditions, which have been lost or dispersed because of the arrival of the white man. The old man's first choice of heirs dies during an initiation ceremony; the second survives. In the end Tata Casehua turns out to be none other than the legendary Yaqui Indian Tetabiate, a veteran who survived the wars between the Yaquis and the Mexican government. This story has been called "an indictment of the white person's way of life," whether the Anglo-

SHORT STORY

American or the Catholic *mestizo* way of life, "which has ignored the indigenous past of the Yaqui and destroyed his oral traditions while oppressing him in body and soul."[1]

Rosa, La Flauta (Rosa, the Flute, 1980), by poet Sergio Elizondo, is a Spanish-language collection of frequently fantastic, sometimes highly personal stories. It consists of ten short pieces, introduced by an *Obertura*, overture, which prepares the reader for the mood and themes he will encounter. The narrative voice in the title work is that of a young girl who gives an account of her years of playing the flute. The story is a reflection on the process of growing up, accommodating to the adult world, and the acceptance of the changes one undergoes. Now that the narrator is a physical adult, she no longer is interested in music, something which once played a large role in her life.

"Pa Que Bailaba Esa Noche" (Why He Danced That Night) concerns a young man who has just moved to a small southwestern desert town. Lonely, he attends a dance where he meets a beautiful young girl. Later, she feels cold as he drives her home, so he lends her his jacket. The next day he discovers that he has forgotten to get it back, and he goes to her house. There he encounters an old woman, the girl's mother, who tells him her daughter has been dead for thirty years. In disbelief the young man accompanies the mother to the cemetery, where his jacket is found hanging on the cross over the dead girl's grave.

The stories in *Rosa, La Flauta* are poetic, sensitive,

and philosophical, yet the author "does not ignore the socioeconomic aspects of Chicano existence," as "his aim seems to be to bring to the surface a whole other reality: the dreams, fantasies and intimate moments in his characters' lives."[2]

In 1982 the acclaimed novelist Rudolfo Anaya published a collection of ten stories, *The Silence of the Llano*. Three are excerpts from his first three novels. Each piece is preceded by an epigraph which introduces a character, sets the scene, or establishes a mood or tone. The title story is about Rafael, a man who lives a lonely life in the harsh New Mexico high country. The narration tells of his parents' cruel winter death, his courting of a village girl, and their subsequent marriage. They lead a beautiful, happy life and she soon gets pregnant. She dies giving birth to a girl. The distraught Rafael leads a virtually silent life for sixteen years. His daughter matures in a world of nature, communicating only with animals. She has contact with people very infrequently until the cruel day when she is raped by a passing stranger. Her father finds her and she calls him by name, an act which causes him to utter his wife's name, Rita, for the first time in sixteen years. Rafael's interest in life is renewed, and he and his daughter begin life together. "The Silence of the Llano" is a powerful story, incorporating the elements of time and nature, full of both the cruelty and the magic of life as it is lived in the plains.

There is much variety in the collection. "The Road to Platero" is similar to the title story, while "The Place of the Swallows" and "The Christmas Play" describe episodes in the lives of rural New Mexican boys. "A Story" and "B. Traven Is Alive and Well in Cuernavaca" are playful fictions about authors and their creations. Both are first-person narratives in which the protagonists are writers. In "A Story" the narrator/writer attends a New Year's Day party where everybody wants to tell a story. This work deals with the writer's creative process, his characters, who also want to get into the story, and much commentary about the craft of fiction. In "B. Traven" the main character, a writer, goes to Cuernavaca, Mexico, to work and meets Justino, a gardener, who tells him a tale of hidden gold. The narrator later meets an elderly, white-haired gentleman, perhaps B. Traven, author of *The Treasure of the Sierra Madre* and a reclusive, almost mythical Mexican figure. The gentleman tells the narrator that he too knew Justino, and that people like him are wonderful sources for literature. The tale ends as the inspired protagonist hurries home because "suddenly the story was overflowing and I needed to write. I needed to get to my quiet room and write the story about B. Traven being alive and well in Cuernavaca."

Some of the tales in *The Adventures of the Chicano Kid and Other Stories*, a 1982 collection by Max Martínez, are accounts of Mexican-American life in small Texas towns or in larger cities such as Houston or San Antonio. The title story carries the subtitle "A Dime Novel" and another heading, "In which the Chicano Kid undertakes a magnificent entrance into the hamlet of Santo Gringo, and of his reception." It is immediately obvious that the story is a parody of the writing of such popular nineteenth-century American novelists as Ned Buntline. The language and tone in Martínez's story are beautifully wrought, ironic duplicates of those in the dime novels:

It was a time of sadness in Santo Gringo, a sadness which swept the territory, leaving it barren of joy and mirth. The morning gently perched itself upon the rooftops of houses and dwellings that long ago verily deserved the signification of home. But that was before the Gringo invaded the territory. Yes, the sun did indeed rise only to shine upon the misery of the doleful Chicano barrio. The velvet blues, the fiery oranges that kissed upon the horizon went unnoticed, as they did each morning, by the denizens of this village of scorn, of abject poverty—reader, if you could only see it! Surely you would be overcome by sympathy and pity. Only the hardest heart of stone could not but melt at such a piteous tableau (7).

The hero here is not John Wayne or the mysterious Lone Ranger of the popular Anglo imagination; instead, he is a perfect, idealized Chicano, a parallel to the perfect Anglos of the literature of the nineteenth and twentieth centuries. The Chicano Kid is a true hero, a bronze-skinned avenger of his race who roams in search of his archenemy Alf Brisket, the despoiler of the Kid's sister. Martínez has created a heroic Old West figure whose duty is to right the wrongs done to his race. The

SHORT STORY

rich language supports the theme, and the ironic tone beautifully reflects the reversal of roles between Mexicans and Anglos found in popular Anglo literature. Martínez uses the weapon of the Anglo against him in order to expose bigotry and uphold the positive values of the Chicanos.

Another story, "Doctor Castillo," is set in modern-day Houston and has nothing to do with Chicanos except for the title character's name. It is a tale of contemporary existence, a sad picture of two characters who reflect the emptiness of urban middle-class life. It also expresses the difficulty of communication and understanding between men and women.

While "Doctor Castillo" could well be about any people, not necessarily Chicanos, and contains nothing racial, "Doña Petra" is quite another matter. This is a chillingly powerful character study of a widow whose husband was killed by *los rinches*, the Texas Rangers. As the story opens, her only son has also just been shot and killed by the same law enforcement officers. After preparations for the funeral, descriptions in which the author masterfully delineates the old woman's resolute strength, she goes to Ranger headquarters and fires three bullets into the man who killed her son. Another Ranger promptly kills her, but "there was a slight smile of contentment on her face." In these three stories and others in his collection Martínez shows himself to be an outstanding stylist and a master of the character study.

Sandra Cisneros is one of a few Chicano writers who have graduated from a creative writing program, in her case the University of Iowa Writer's Workshop. She is distinctive also in that she is a native of the Midwest, Chicago, where she grew up among Puerto Ricans. She wrote many poems and short prose pieces that appeared in magazines and anthologies before the publication in 1983 of *The House on Mango Street*, a work she completed as a National Endowment for the Arts Fellow. In 1985 *Mango Street* won the Before Columbus American Book Award. It is dedicated "A las mujeres/ To The Women" and contains forty-four short passages, some only a paragraph or two in length. The narrative voice is that of a child named Esperanza, who gives accounts of events and people in her urban environment. The book could well be classified as a novel, since Esperanza provides the necessary novelistic unity in her record of feelings about her world.

In "My Name," Esperanza thinks, as do all children, about her name, but a Chicana must think of its significance in two languages: "In English my name means hope. In Spanish it means too many letters. It means sadness, it means waiting. It is like the number nine. A muddy color. It is the Mexican records my father plays on Sunday mornings when he is shaving, songs like sobbing" (12). In this passage Cisneros demonstrates her talent for creating multiple meanings through simple imagery. In another piece with the intriguing title of "The Earl of Tennessee," Esperanza describes Earl, a jukebox repairman who speaks with a southern accent, smokes fat cigars, wears a felt hat, and gives everyone phonograph records. "What Sally Said" is a chilling account of child abuse, while "Those Who

Don't" contrasts the comfort people feel in their own neighborhoods, among their own race, with the fear they experience in other sections of the city among people of another color. *The House on Mango Street* is, finally, an account of the development of a writer; in the last story, "Mango Says Goodbye Sometimes," the narrator writes: "I like to tell stories. I am going to tell you a story about a girl who didn't want to belong. . . . I put it down on paper and then the ghost does not ache too much" (101). Cisneros's collection is a captivating account of memories of growing up in a Chicano world, and expresses the need to recover the past in order in accept the present.

Gary D. Keller, who holds a PhD degree from Columbia University, was the founder and director of the prominent Chicano publishing firm Bilingual Press/ Editorial Bilingüe. Keller writes fiction and poetry under the pseudonym of El Huitlacoche, the name of a real Mexican boxer of the 1950s ("I know him as a boxer I admired some years ago who being a poor Indian became wealthy with his fists and returned wealth to the poor"),[3] and it is Huitlacoche who narrates and appears in the short stories.

Keller's collection of stories, *Tales of El Huitlacoche* (1984), provides a contrast to Cisneros's work, as the four stories in his volume are humorous and frequently cynical views of U.S. society. "Papi Invented the Automatic Jumping Bean" is about a man who takes a cold capsule and some mercury from a thermometer and invents the classic child's toy. This is merely the latest in a long list of Papi's efforts to acquire money as he seeks to better his sons' lives through the earnings from his inventions. Predictably, the secret of the jumping bean is stolen and marketed by others (Anglos, presumably), so the family receives not a dime. The sons succeed in college, and, after the father's death, the narrator thinks of him with mixed emotions, including forgiving him his failures, laying the blame on a "myopic, racist society that would have granted a white Anglo of his talents an adequate station in life" (9). The tale concludes with a question: "Why wasn't Papi recognized as the inventor of the wormless bean and other joyous novelties?" (11).

"Mocha in Disneyland" is about a Chicano college professor, divorced from his Anglo wife, and their son, Pancholín, sometimes called Mocha because he is of mixed blood, thus the color of *café con leche* (coffee with milk). The professor (El Huitlacoche) takes his son to Disneyland, where they spend the night illegally in a treehouse. Much of their discussion revolves around the story of the Golden Carp, a myth of the origin of the Chicano people, which derives from Rudolfo Anaya's novel *Bless Me, Última*. There is also a conversation about the boy's heritage and the use of the racial terms "Chicano" and "Gabacho." As the protagonist recalls events in his life, there is a portrait of a successful, middle-class Chicano struggling to survive in an Anglo world. Critic Rosaura Sánchez has said that the outstanding feature of Keller's stories is a

burlesque style and a comic vision that serve to reveal the absurdity of human existence and the

SHORT STORY

contradictions of society. . . . Throughout the stories,
El Huitlacoche has chosen to focus on the impact of
various social and economic contradictions on the
individual through the use of exaggeration, grotesque
descriptions, and humorous discourse. Thus, while
externalizing fears, repressions, and human bodily
acts, the author exposes social conventions, racist/class
relations, capitalist labor practices, and the exploitation
of undocumented workers in every sphere of American
society.[4]

The Iguana Killer: Twelve Stories of the Heart, by Alberto Alvaro Ríos, was the winner of the 1984 Western
States Book Award for short fiction in the year of its
publication. The author is a professor of English, and
has published several highly respected volumes of poetry. Although much of his short fiction has appeared in
journals such as the *Revista Chicano-Riqueña* and *De Col-
ores: The Best of Chicano Fiction*, this is his first collection.
The title story is about a young boy named Sapito (Little
Toad) who lives in the town of Villahermosa, in the
tropics of Mexico's isthmus. His grandmother, who
lives in Nogales, Arizona, gives the boy a baseball bat
one Christmas. Knowing nothing of the sport, Sapito
uses his gift for something he and all the boys of his
area do know, killing iguanas, a local food staple. "The
Iguana Killer" is a sensitive, well-drawn character study
of a Mexican boy who sees his first snow on a visit to
his grandmother's, and at the end of the story makes a
crib from the shell of a giant sea turtle. He leaves his gift
at the doorstep of the mother of a newborn infant.

"The Child" is a finely written story of two elderly women friends traveling by bus from Guaymas, Mexico, to Nogales, Arizona, for the funeral of one's brother. During a meal stop they discover a dead child, but the father, with whom they had conversed after he told them the child was ill, is nowhere to be seen. He had said that he was en route to the United States to see a medical specialist. The chilling conclusion to the story is the discovery that the boy has long been dead, his intestines removed and replaced with bags of opium. There is a splendid stylistic counterpoint at work in this story as Ríos's narrative refers to nonverbal communication. For example, Mrs. García and Mrs. Sandoval are long-time friends who "sometimes would shake their heads, and this said all the words" (13). This attention to *how* people communicate extends to other characters as well; the police sergeant, for instance, investigating the dead body starts out communicating "from the mouth, like a sergeant," but his tone softens so "he was a man after all." The story ends on a similar note: "Oh my God, *Dios mío, Dios mío* was all Mrs. Sandoval kept saying, maybe with words, saying just like Mrs. García. Their heads moved from side to side, but not fast enough" (21).

Most of the other stories are like "The Iguana Killer" in that they feature children and deal with the rites of growing up—some strictly Chicano experiences, most of them universal. All of the tales give evidence of a talented prose stylist with a fine hand for characterization and an ear well tuned to duplicating dialogue. All are in English, sprinkled with Spanish words and expressions. In most cases Ríos strives to accentuate the positive aspects of Chicano or Mexican life as people go about the everyday business of existence.

Helena María Viramontes, in her collection *The Moths and Other Stories* (1985), is a writer whose short stories depict with vivid reality the lives of Mexican-American women. "The Moths" is about a teen-age tomboy who has trouble getting along with her family—sisters, mother, and father. Since the only person who understands the girl is her grandmother, the two spend a lot of time together. The old woman dies at the story's end, and the moths of her soul fly from her mouth, "fluttering to light, circling the single dull bulb of the bathroom" (28). As the girl weeps for her dead grandmother, she also weeps for the loss of her childhood and for the harsh role she must play as an adult woman. Her sisters and her mother have all succumbed to male-dominated existence in the Chicano world, but the protagonist may not share their fate since she has previously defied both her father and the Catholic Church, the latter by refusing to attend and the former even after his tirades about her not going to mass. She has shown resistance to two of the major forces which work to keep women in their traditionally submissive roles.

"Snapshots" is a first-person narration by Olga Ruiz, a divorced woman who spent thirty years in the boring, deadly routines of life as a housewife and mother. Now that her husband is gone and she is alien-

UNDERSTANDING CHICANO LITERATURE

ated from her adult daughter, Olga spends days poring over old photographs in a family album. Her interior monologues reveal her reactions to long years of repetitive housecleaning. She also muses about sex and passion, and she expresses relief over the diminution of her husband's passion during the course of their marriage. She searches the snapshots for meaning in her life, but realizes that the pictures are not real; they are only fleeting moments in time. As the tale closes, she thinks her grandmother may have been right—photographs do steal people's souls: "It scares me . . . to think I don't have a snapshot of her. If I find one, I'll tear it up for sure" (99).

Viramontes's style in all eight of the stories is varied, with interior monologue, shifting viewpoints, and some presentation of nonlinear time. Her adeptness at quick, efficient characterization is displayed in portraits of people of all ages, from adolescents to grandmothers, and the men that appear in her work are deftly drawn.

The subtitle of *Living Up the Street* (1985), by Gary Soto, describes the theme of his volume of short prose. It is, indeed, twenty-one "Narrative Recollections" of the life of one of contemporary Chicano poetry's most respected voices. The world Soto presents is that of a boy growing up in Fresno, California, his experiences in the *barrio*, in school, in church, and with girls. There are also glimpses of the adult writer.

"Baseball in April" is about the narrator and his brother, boys who are enthusiastic about baseball in the early spring. After failing to make the local little league teams, they practice hard and play a few games with other boys in a makeshift league, but by the time school is out everyone has gradually drifted away and there is no more baseball, only television. Another tale, "Black Hair," also the title of one of Soto's volumes of poetry, is the story of a seventeen-year-old narrator who has run away to Glendale and gotten a job hauling automobile tires in a factory. It is dirty, demanding physical labor. Most of his co-workers are illegal Mexicans or blacks, with a few "redneck whites" in the group. The narrator and main character is different from them all, a *pocho* who speaks bad Spanish. Among the lessons he learns during this work experience is that the world is indifferent to the plight of the individual who exists on the fringes of society. He begins to appreciate the rough life of an undocumented worker, with its risks and uncertainties, but still he realizes that "few quit; no one was ever fired. It amazed me that no one gave up when the border patrol jumped from their vans, baton in hand, because I couldn't imagine any work that could be worse—or any life. What was out there, in the world, that made men run for the fence in fear?" (120). *Living Up the Street* won the 1985 American Book Award.

The Cat and Other Stories (1986), by Beverly Silva, contains opening and closing tales about cats, while the thirteen pieces in between deal with graduate student life, politics, love, children, friendship, and daily experiences in large and small California towns. Most of her work here is personal, and narration is in the first person. Several are nostalgic, sometimes with a mixture of bitterness and sadness. "Smile," for example, is a short selection treating an episode in the life of a divorced woman who is forced to send her uncontrollable teen-age daughter to a juvenile home. At the close of the narration the girl chooses to live with her father, whom she hates. "Smile" ends with "I stopped smiling after that. Learning to cry was difficult. Learning how to use the tears was even more difficult. But I did learn how to save my smiles for very special occasions" (49). Silva is also a poet, with a 1983 collection, *The Second St. Poems.*

A recently published collection, *The Last of the Menu Girls* (1986), is by New Mexican writer Denise Chávez. Since the seven narratives all have the same protago-nist, Rocío, the book has been referred to as a novel. *Menu Girls* traces the development of a young woman from the time of her earliest rebellion against the tradi-tional roles imposed on her by society through her de-velopment of a will to become a novelist, inspired to write about her family and surroundings.

The title story is about Rocío's experiences with her first summer job as a hospital aide who brings menu cards to patients' rooms each morning for them to select their meals for the following day. As she visits her pa-tients, Chicano and Anglo, those recuperating and those dying, the protagonist grows, learns, and ma-tures: "My heart reached out to every person, dragged itself through the hallways with the patients, cried when they did, laughed when they did. I had no busi-ness in the job. I was too emotional" (35). After return-ing to school Rocío is in a traffic accident and becomes a patient at the hospital where she worked. She discovers that the administrators have changed the cafeteria sys-

SHORT STORY

tem and there are no more menu girls. In *The Last of the Menu Girls*, Denise Chávez reveals a talent for nostalgia, humor, and irony. Her novel/short story collection provides a fine perspective on the condition of a young Chicana as she struggles with her life.

Before concluding this survey of Chicano short fiction, it must be observed that the works of many fine writers have not been discussed. The extreme popularity of the genre and the overwhelming number of published stories makes a full, comprehensive treatment here impossible. A glance at the tables of contents of only one quarterly journal—*The Americas Review* (formerly the *Revista Chicano-Riqueña*)—will reveal that each issue contains many *cuentos*; thus in more than fifteen years of just this one publication hundreds of writers have seen their work in print. Anthologies such as *Best New Chicano Literature 1986* or *Palabra Nueva* show that new *cuentistas* are appearing on the scene rapidly, and that established writers such as Ron Arias, Rudolfo Anaya, Rosaura Sánchez, and Rolando Hinojosa-Smith are regular contributors to the genre. This brief discussion can only be a starting point for those wishing to experience the wonders of the Chicano world through the medium of the short story.

Notes

1. Oscar Urquídez-Somoza and Julio A. Martínez, "Miguel Méndez M.," *Chicano Literature: A Reference Guide*, ed. Julio A. Martínez and Francisco A. Lomelí. (Westport CT: Greenwood Press, 1985) 271.

2. Charles M. Tatum, *Chicano Literature.* (Boston: Twayne, 1982) 95.

3. Gary D. Keller, "The Mojado Who Offered Up His Tapeworms to the Public Weal," *Tales of El Huitlacoche.* (Colorado Springs: Maize Press, 1984) 13.

4. Rosaura Sánchez, "The Comic Vision in *Tales of El Huitlacoche,*" introduction, *Tales of El Huitlacoche* vii–viii.

CHAPTER 5

Autobiography

In any discussion of the development of Chicano prose fiction the importance of memoirs and chronicles of exploration must be considered for their role in laying the groundwork for the modern novel and short story. Critic Luis Leal has discussed the significance of nonfiction writing that he calls "didactic"—memoirs, diaries, chronicles, accounts of trips, narratives, letters—in Chicano literature prior to 1900, and has concluded that modern critics need to reexamine those works for the purposes of establishing firmer foundations for the general history of Chicano literature.[1] Moreover, contemporary autobiography, even though the corpus of publications is still rather small, needs to be studied for a complete understanding of the totality of Chicano writing.

The first modern autobiography was that of Ernesto Galarza (1905–1984), a scholar and historian who wrote *Merchants of Labor: The Mexican Bracero Story* (1964), one of the most important books about agriculture in the United States. Galarza's novelistic memoir, *Barrio Boy*

(1971), traces his life from his early years in the Mexican mountain village where he was born, through his family's flight from the chaos of the 1910 revolution, to their settling in Sacramento, California. At book's end the author is a student in high school.

In a brief preface to his autobiography Galarza tells the reader that it had its beginnings as "anecdotes I told my family about Jalcocotán, the mountain village . . . where I was born." But the work grew to become a historical account and psychological image of all Mexican immigrants. The psychological portrait Galarza paints is his effort to offset the damage done by many psychologists, psychiatrists, social anthropologists, and others who, in Galarza's words, "have spread the rumor that these Mexican immigrants and their offspring have lost their 'self-image.' By this, of course, they mean that a Mexican doesn't know what he is; and if by chance he is something, it isn't any good."

In the last chapter, "On the Edge of the Barrio," young Galarza is reaching a new maturity. He has had to face family death, job responsibilities, school, and the realization that he is unique. He begins to work in a migrant camp, observes that the conditions are deplorable, attempts to organize the laborers, and is fired for his efforts. Ernesto knows that he can go back to school, but most of his fellow Chicanos are trapped in the migratory routine, doomed to a life of stoop labor and poor pay.

Much of Chicano literature is highly personal, sometimes only thinly disguised as fiction. *The Autobi-*

AUTOBIOGRAPHY

ography of a Brown Buffalo (1972), by the mysterious Oscar Zeta Acosta, presents a vastly different kind of life story from Galarza's straightforward autobiography. Acosta's *Autobiography* and its sequel, *The Revolt of the Cockroach People* (1973), are almost always classified as novels, but are included here because of their autobiographical nature. They are at the same time a blend of fact and product of the writer's pure imagination.

Acosta was a Texan, born in El Paso in 1936, but his family moved to California when he was still young. After a troubled youth he finished high school, served in the U.S. Air Force, and attended college. After college he attended law school part-time, passing the bar exam in 1966. A few years after writing his "novels," Acosta disappeared; no one has seen or heard from him since 1974.

The Autobiography of a Brown Buffalo features a protagonist searching for his identity. He leaves his job as a big city lawyer, travels throughout the Southwest, and experiments with drugs and alcohol. At the end of a six-month odyssey he winds up in the Mexican border city of Juárez, where he discovers himself and begins to take pride in his Chicano heritage. The racial and cultural significance of the title becomes evident, for "brown buffalo" suggests both the skin color of many Chicanos and their threatened extinction:

We are all citizens by default. They stole our land and made us half-slaves. They destroyed our land and made us bow down to a dead man who's been strung

UNDERSTANDING CHICANO LITERATURE

up for 2000 years. . . . Now what we need is, first to give ourselves a new name. We need a new identity. A name and a language all our own. . . . So I propose that we call ourselves . . . the Brown Buffalo people. . . . The buffalo, see? Yes, the animal that everyone slaughtered. Sure, both the cowboys and the Indians are out to get him . . . and, because we do have roots in our Mexican past, our Aztec ancestry, that's where we get the *brown* from (198).

In *The Revolt of the Cockroach People* the now proud and defiant protagonist sets himself up as a legal counsel in Los Angeles, where he champions the causes of Chicanos and other downtrodden peoples. In almost cinematic fashion *Revolt* covers the complicated social and political period of 1968–1970 in California, a time of great unrest among the Chicanos in Los Angeles. Included among the characters, either named directly or thinly disguised, are such prominent figures as Mayor Sam Yorty, César Chávez, Ronald Reagan, Robert Kennedy, and Rubén Salazar, a Chicano journalist killed during the 1970 national Chicano moratorium against the Vietnam war. The protagonist/narrator adopts the name Zeta in order to evoke Mexican revolutionary heroes of the 1910 struggle, especially Emiliano Zapata, the champion of the poor. The cockroaches of the title are a direct allusion to the famous song of the revolution, "La Cucaracha." At the end, like the real-life Oscar Zeta Acosta, the protagonist in the two-volume autobiography/novel disappears forever. His personal

AUTOBIOGRAPHY

struggle has been suspended for a while, perhaps forever.

Few writers have provoked as much controversy among Mexican-Americans as Richard Rodriguez. His 1982 autobiography entitled *Hunger of Memory: The Education of Richard Rodriguez* has been vigorously attacked by Chicanos while, interestingly, highly praised in such mainstream publications as the *New York Times Book Review* and *Newsweek*. A single reason explains the two divergent opinions: *Hunger of Memory* is based on an assimilationist posture which also rejects bilingual education. But Rodriguez's autobiography is undisputedly a finely written, sensitive portrayal of the power of language. In the prologue, entitled "Middle Class Pastoral," the author defines the subject of his work: it is "a book about language. . . . Language has been the great subject of my life."

The book's six chapters describe a life defined by language, the "private" one of home and family—Spanish—and the "public" one of society and success—English. Rodriguez recounts a childhood characterized by an acute awareness of sounds. Images of how he and his family sounded in both languages inform his memories of his early years. His pronouncements about the detriments of bilingual education are deeply rooted in the child's personality he reveals and in a belief in the importance of "public individuality." He says:

Today I hear bilingual educators say that children lose a degree of "individuality" by becoming assimilated into public society. . . . But the bilingualists . . . do not seem to realize that there are *two* ways a person is individualized. So they do not realize that while one suffers a diminished sense of *private* individuality by becoming assimilated into public society, such assimilation makes possible the achievement of *public* individuality (26).

Richard speaks Spanish until he goes to school, where his teachers suggest that he should speak only English, both at home and at school. This forces a wedge between him and the intimacy he has known within his family and forever changes his life. English, the language of the *gringos*, spoken in halting, accented tones at first, becomes the medium through which he succeeds in university studies, as a scholar and as a writer of autobiography.

Hunger of Memory has an element of the literary confession about it. Rodriguez explains the alienation he felt from Chicano activists and makes clear his disregard for Affirmative Action and other programs for minority students. Yet he passed through the doors that opened for him *because* he was Hispanic. In a passage that refers poignantly to the lack of educational advantages for the poor, he says: "You who read this act of contrition should know that by writing it I seek a kind of forgiveness—not yours. The forgiveness, rather, of those many persons whose absence from higher education permitted me to be classed a minority student" (153).

AUTOBIOGRAPHY

The severe criticism that this autobiography has drawn from many Mexican-American writers and critics has focused on his rejection of sociopolitical ideals and programs, a rejection that appears to threaten the moral authority of the Civil Rights Movement. The importance of this work does not lie in its messages, however. *Hunger of Memory* is the artistic representation of a life which has found both meaning and expression in language, and it should be considered a stylistic standard for future Chicano autobiography.

Note

1. Luis Leal; "Cuatro Siglos de Prosa Aztlanse," *Aztlán y México: Perfiles literarios e históricos* (Binghamton, NY: Bilingual Press/Editorial Bilingüe, 1985) 60.

CHAPTER 6

Literatura Chicanesca

Literatura Chicanesca, or literature about Chicanos by non-Chicanos, is a fascinating and sometimes controversial consideration in any discussion of Chicano literature. The term was first used in 1976 by Francisco A. Lomelí and Donaldo W. Urioste in *Chicano Perspectives in Literature: A Critical and Annotated Bibliography.* They contend that

the uniqueness of Chicano reality is such that non-Chicanos rarely capture it like it is. For this reason, we propose [their] efforts to be termed *literatura chicanesca* because it only appears to be Chicano. Therefore, it must be kept in mind that the perspective is from the outside looking in. This perspective loses the spontaneity of a natural outpouring of a people's subconscious through the writer's creativity; instead, it becomes a calculated object of study which is valued from a relative distance, that is, not lived.[1]

LITERATURA CHICANESCA

The term is new, but the depiction of Chicanos or Mexicans in the literature of the United States is not. Cecil Robinson, in his comprehensive study *With the Ears of Strangers: The Mexican in American Literature,*[2] traces the subject from the earliest fictional descriptions of encounters between Mexican and Anglo cultures in the Southwest up to the 1960s. In a revised and expanded version of his first work, *Mexico and the Hispanic Southwest in American Literature,* Robinson presents an argument in favor of the perspective of an outsider, a knowledgeable observer writing about people unlike himself, who can be theoretically detached from his subject and therefore has the "advantage of a double vision, the view from within and the view from without."[3] Many other scholars, however, feel that *literatura chicanesca* fails to present Chicano life and culture in an honest or realistic manner. For example, Antonio Márquez says that it has "remained a promise and has largely failed to adequately depict the Chicano experience."[4] Perhaps the main reason so many critics reject *literatura chicanesca* is that a negative stereotype of the Mexican and Mexican-American has been perpetrated in "mainstream" writing since the first quarter of the nineteenth century. This is an unfair result of the clash between two cultures with vastly different value systems. As the Protestant Anglo moved westward, encountered the Catholic Mexican and observed his "alien" ways, literature portrayed a "good" Anglo versus "bad" Mexican conflict.

UNDERSTANDING CHICANO LITERATURE

In modern times there have been quite a few Anglo authors who have presented Chicanos in a more realistic fashion. Prominent examples include Paul Horgan (*The Common Heart*, 1942), Oliver LaFarge (*Behind the Mountains*, 1956), and the prolific Frank Waters (*People of the Valley*, 1941). Waters's novel is an accurate and fair portrait of New Mexican Hispanic people. It is the story of a *curandera*, a faith-healer akin to Última in Rudolfo Anaya's *Bless Me, Última.* The protagonist, Maria del Valle, is the daughter of an Indian woman who died giving birth. The girl grows up tending flocks of goats, and is a child as wild as her charges. She learns to live with nature and understand its ways. As an adult Maria has a child by a *gringo* soldier; later she has other children by other men and soon becomes a grandmother. Now skilled as a *curandera*, she is near eighty when she hears of a government proposal to build a dam in her valley. As a wise, respected leader of the people, she opposes the project. She stands before a local judge, explaining that she does not oppose the dam and everything new that it represents; rather she upholds the old ways of her people. In a clear, simple, effective style Frank Waters offers the reader an unforgettable picture of a living representative of the unique and beautiful Hispanic way of life in northern New Mexico.

In 1972 Eugene Nelson published a fictionalized account of the struggles of Mexican migrant workers. *The Bracero* deals with the efforts of Nacho Ramírez, a young man from southern Mexico, to earn enough money to support his family. His only ambition is to work, but the desperate conditions of life in his country doom him to poverty if he remains there. As a consequence he sets out to become a *bracero*, a temporary worker in the United States. After an odyssey up the west coast of his homeland, Nacho is crossing the border when it is discovered that he has tuberculosis. He is denied papers, left penniless, sick and dying, one of many victims of poverty south of the border.

Critic Antonio Márquez has called Nelson's novel respectable, "with an energetic narrative line, strong characters and an engaging theme." He concludes that it is "more successful than some Chicano novels . . . in depicting and dramatizing the travails of the *bracero*."[5] The novel is a realistic treatment of the subject, and a strong indictment of a deplorable social situation that has existed between Mexico and the United States for many years. It is marred, however, by serious stylistic flaws. In his attempt to duplicate the rhythms and nuances of Mexican speech, Nelson created a false-sounding, inauthentic English dialogue, which at best is distracting. The author has also treated the same subject in nonfiction, in his 1975 documentary book *Pablo Cruz and the American Dream*, a transcription of interviews with an undocumented immigrant from Mexico.

One of the most popular and successful modern writers who have attempted to write about Chicanos is John Nichols. He was already an established author (*The Sterile Cuckoo*, 1965) when he published his New Mexico trilogy, consisting of *The Milagro Beanfield War* (1974), *The Magic Journey* (1978), and *The Nirvana Blues*

(1981). The first is the best of the three. The war referred to in the title begins when the main character, Joe Mondragón, illegally opens an irrigation ditch onto his land in order to water his beans. Because of the constant problem in the western states over water rights and land claims, Joe's act is a defiant and significant one which provides the impetus for conflicts in the novel. The floodgates of the author's imagination are also opened, and the reader witnesses an array of colorful Chicano characters, ranging from Amarante Córdova, called the "human zipper" because of his many operations, to the wild, one-armed Onofre Martínez, who drives around in a battered truck with a three-legged German shepherd perched on the roof of the cab.

Nichols's singular talent creates an original blend of myth and reality in his imaginary world. Martínez is the source of modern legend, since every strange or unexplained happening is said to be caused by "El brazo Onofre," the missing arm, which, according to Martínez, fell off one day, releasing a huge cloud of crimson butterflies. Other characters achieve mythic proportions; the real merges with the fantastic, legend with history, and the ever-present social conflict provides the narrative movement. The beanfield becomes the symbol of the Chicano's plight in New Mexico: lost water rights, lost lands, and exploitation by Anglo outsiders. Wealthy developer Ladd Devine is the symbol of white conglomerates taking over the Chicano people of the valley and destroying an irreplaceable way of life. *The Milagro Beanfield War* is Nichols at his best; the novel vibrates with the wonder and the woe of Chicano existence in the Southwest.

The Magic Journey, set in Chamisaville near Milagro, spans the years between the Great Depression and the early 1970s. The Anglo villain here is Dale Rodey Mc-Queen, who drives into town in a beat-up yellow schoolbus loaded with dynamite. The blacksmith, Cipi García, tries to repair the bus, but it explodes, and he emerges from the rubble while "tiny particles . . . no larger than pollen flakes settled like a fine, golden gauze onto the crater floor." García is "clad only in boots, and holding, in one hand, a single rose." Later, when hot springs begin to flow from the crater, the spot is declared a shrine to the "Dynamite Virgin" and entrepreneurs move in to reap the profits by developing a tourist attraction with hotels, bathhouses, and restaurants. McQueen is the first of a long line of developers, politicians, and speculators intent on amassing money at the expense of the Chicanos. *The Magic Journey* eventually focuses on McQueen's daughter, April Delaney, an exceptionally well-drawn character who embodies a 1960s radical leader. She is killed in another dynamite blast as her father and other Anglo schemers at last succeed in "pizza-fying America," as Nichols later described it. The work ends on an optimistic note, however, as Chicano old-timers gather for April's symbolic funeral. The last line, "They had work to do," (566), reaffirms the revolutionary theme and points to a continuing struggle. *The Magic Journey* has been hailed by some critics as a major revolutionary novel. In it,

Nichols demonstrates a high degree of understanding of the Chicanos who populate his work. He has chosen to bear their standard, and he does so with integrity and sympathy. There is no question that he is an eloquent, knowledgeable spokesman for the Chicano people who are rapidly losing their land, their cultural identity, and their ancient, traditional way of life.

The Nirvana Blues is set in Chamisaville and has an Anglo protagonist, Joe Miniver. While struggling to keep his failing marriage alive he has resorted to a dope-smuggling enterprise as a maneuver to acquire sufficient funds to buy a small plot of land from Eloy Irribarrén, "The Last Chicano." Like the other two novels *The Nirvana Blues* is comic, but there is an underlying sense of sadness and despair at the uncontrollable and inevitable circumstances that lead to the death of Eloy and his way of life. While *The Milagro Beanfield War* and *The Magic Journey* both end on hopeful notes, the last part of the trilogy ends with death: both Joe and "The last Chicano" are defeated, killed as a result of rampant capitalism. Nichols's view of the Chicano's fate in modern America is a pessimistic one, but his portrayal of the Mexican-American in his work has been called "exemplary," a model that provides a "direction that literatura chicanesca must take if it is to . . . be of significant value."[6]

In recent years there has been a new twist to *literatura chicanesca*: a few non-Chicanos are not only writing about Chicanos, they are pretending to *be* Chicanos, publishing their work under assumed names and false identities. Chester Seltzer (1915–1971), an Anglo newswpaperman, wrote short fiction under a variation of his wife's name (Amado Muro), and his stories were published in such journals as the *Arizona Quarterly* and the *Southwest Review*. Most critics are not happy with Seltzer's deception, condemning the author while at the same time praising the verisimilitude in his stories. Some pass it off as a "gentle" deception; his ploy has been explained as one to avoid personal attention more than to deceive. Some conclude that he did not wish to trade on his father's name—Louis B. Seltzer, famed editor of the *Cleveland Press* and chief editor for the Scripps-Howard papers in Ohio. The fact that the author was married to a Mexican may, in the minds of many, make him by extension part of the Chicano fold. His identity notwithstanding, his stories were well received, with at least seven appearing in *The Best American Short Stories*. An editor of one anthology (published before Seltzer's true identity was widely known) included "Cecilia Rosas" and stated in the introduction that Muro "seems to have written more good short fiction than any other young Mexican American."[7] Muro/Seltzer sometimes wrote about rootless men on the move in search of work in the Southwest; more frequently he portrayed the lives of Mexicans and Mexican-Americans living in the Texas and New Mexico borderlands. His stories are written in a spare style that has been compared to that of Ernest Hemingway.

"Cecilia Rosas" is a humorous, sympathetic portrayal of a love-starved fourteen-year-old Chicano boy called Amado Muro. The object of his affection is the woman of the title, a twenty-year-old sales clerk in an El Paso department store where they both work. She is described as beautiful, but she also "prided herself on being more American than Mexican because she was born in El Paso. And she did her best to act, dress, and talk the way Americans do. She hated to speak Spanish, disliked her Mexican name" (71). The story concludes as Amado, after having been the butt of her joke (she stands him up on a date she requests and instead goes out with an Anglo) learns a lesson in love and in life.

Even though Seltzer was not a Chicano, his fiction presents Chicanos realistically, both in detail and in spirit. His success as a "Chicano" writer has been praised:

His artistic ability with language is only surpassed by his complete depiction of the *barrio.* The main threads of Chicano culture—the values, customs, beliefs and language of the people—run consistently and accurately throughout his *barrio* stories, more so than in the work of any other American writer who chose to depict Mexicans and their culture. Seltzer aesthetically expressed the world and experience of Amada Muro, and in so doing, Seltzer really did become Amado Muro, a Mexican from Chihuahua.[8]

Danny Santiago and his novel *Famous All Over Town* (1983) made the front page of the *New York Times* in 1984 when it was revealed that the author is not the young Chicano writer he had pretended to be. He is Daniel James, an Anglo and a 1933 Yale graduate with a degree in classical Greek. He was a prize-winning playwright and screenwriter (in 1944 he collaborated with his wife, Lilith, in writing *Bloomer Girl*, which played on Broadway for almost two years). His knowledge of Chicano life comes from his twenty years in a Los Angeles *barrio* where he was a volunteer worker. James claims that he assumed a Chicano identity not to deceive, but because he believed that he had been blacklisted after he was named as a member of the Communist Party in 1951 by the House Un-American Activities Committee. Danny Santiago is not the first pseudonym he has employed; in the 1950s he wrote horror movies under the name of Daniel Hyatt. There has been great hue and cry over James's impersonation of a Chicano, but *Famous All Over Town* has nevertheless been hailed by some as a classic of the Chicano urban experience.

The novel began as a short story, "The Somebody," which first appeared in *Redbook* magazine in 1970. It met with immediate success, and was widely anthologized in ethnic and Chicano collections. It became a staple in Chicano literature classes and was chosen to be included in *Best American Short Stories*. "The Somebody" later became (in an altered form) the first chapter of the novel. *Famous All Over Town* is narrated by fourteen-year-old Rudy "Chato" Medina, an intelligent boy who struggles to maintain his identity in the face of many pressures, both within his family and in society. The language in the novel is reminiscent of J. D. Salinger's *Catcher in the Rye* as Chato's wry, verbal humor reveals a tough, cynical boy while also revealing unpleasant truths about the Chicano world: "My father is very loud in stores speaking Spanish, but in English you can barely hear him." *Famous All Over Town* depicts a community and a family in upheaval: as the Southern Railway destroys the neighborhood, the family falls apart. In the end Chato is arrested for writing his name on walls, but he emerges from jail with the will and desire to become a writer, to be "somebody," to tell his tale.

The novel was well received, with laudatory reviews in the *New York Times Book Review*, the *Los Angeles Times*, and *USA Today*. It was selected for the Rosenthal Award, an annual prize for both painters and writers, presented by the American Academy and Institute of Arts and Letters. The prize is for fiction which, though not a commercial success, is a considerable literary achievement. Partially as a result of this event, Danny Santiago's true identity became known, and after the hoax was revealed, the novel suddenly took on significance more as a social document than as a work of fiction. Daniel James has said of his pose, however, that he feels more comfortable writing as Danny Santiago, that he in effect becomes Santiago as he writes and is better for it: "He's so much freer than I am myself. He seems to know how he feels about everything and none of the ifs, ands and buts that I'm plagued with."[9]

In spite of problems of identity and deception, both Chester Seltzer and Daniel James immersed themselves so thoroughly in Chicano culture that they emerged as new people, Amado Muro and Danny Santiago. Their writings ring true; they are expertly wrought, sensitive, and realistic portraits of the people and places of Chicano communities. The authors were not Chicanos; their works are examples of *literatura chicanesca* at its best.

Another writer who has immersed himself in Chicano culture and written successfully about it is Jim Sagel. He is not a Chicano (his parents were Russian immigrants), but Sagel was born in Colorado and is married to a Mexican-American woman. As an instructor in bilingual language and literature, Sagel also speaks and writes Spanish. His collection of short stories, *Tunomás Honey* (1983), won the Cuban Premio Casa de las Américas award in 1981 for the original Spanish version.

The pieces in *Tunomás Honey* are set in northern New Mexico, near the town of Española, where the author resides and works. They deal with the old, traditional Hispanic residents of the area (*manitos*) and depict their life style, which frequently conflicts with the ways of the younger generation. In the author's note at the beginning of the bilingual collection (translations by Sagel), he states that he has attempted to capture, in the Spanish version, "the local sound and flavor of the Spanish spoken in northern New Mexico. This is one of a very few books written to date in northern New Mexican dialect."

The title story is a character study of an old bachelor

with the nickname "Tunomás Honey." He has an eye for the ladies and is accustomed to telling all of them the same: "You are the only one, Honey," which is what they call him. He is constantly in trouble with the women of the area, both married and single. "El Americano" is about a Chicano, Darryl Francis Galvan, given the name "El Americano" by his relatives because he doesn't speak "mexicano." All his life Darryl has been in trouble and never felt he belonged with others. He attends Fairview High School, a private academy, which

skimmed off all the Anglos in the community who didn't want to go to the public schools with the Mexicans and Indians. And the few Chicanos who did attend Fairview High were obligated to leave their culture, customs, and accents outside, like shoes at the door. It was a place where they scrubbed down la Raza until they shone whiter than the finest china (30).

Since Darryl is bookish and effeminate, his father, who is worried about his own reputation, sends him away from home every summer to work on his relatives' ranch. The boy hates the work, detests the living conditions, and cannot tolerate the food. The story convincingly presents a contrast between generations and depicts one person's complete acculturation by one culture and alienation from another. Darryl has become an Anglo.

LITERATURA CHICANESCA

Sagel is also a poet, with several published collections, among them *Los cumpleaños de doña Agueda* (Doña Agueda's Birthday), published in 1984. Chicano novelist Rudolfo Anaya wrote the introduction to this work, praising the author for his

perceptiveness of the people he observes in the multilingual community of Española and its environment. The style is direct, crisp, and concrete, but there is also a sense of patience which is always inherent in a good storyteller. The language is the language of the Hispanos del norte [of the north], the patois of the native speaker, flowing easily from Spanish to English, and the blends in between. The language captures the flavor of life.[10]

Jim Sagel is a writer who completely understands the people about whom he writes, both in prose and in poetry. His admiration and love for them is apparent in all his work.

The Mexican and the Chicano have long been popular subjects for the pens of Anglo writers in the United States. Some have been so attracted to Hispanic life here that they have even pretended to be Mexican-Americans, publishing their work under false identities. Antonio Márquez has made the point that any writer who chooses to practice *literatura chicanesca* is obliged to be "knowledgeable, honest, intrepid, uncompromising, and above all—true." He goes on to explain that the writer "has to explore the Chicano experience in its intricate manifestations—the good and the bad, the noble and the ignoble, and render the perplexities, paradoxes, and complex cultural, social and political situations that animate Chicano life and culture."[11] In the early years of American literature the portrait of the Mexican and his Chicano cousin generally was degrading and stereotypical, anything but knowledgeable and honest. Through such masters of *literatura chicanesca* as John Nichols, Amado Muro/Chester Seltzer, and Jim Sagel, one can enjoy prose and poetry that capture the unique experience of being a Chicano, with realistic presentations of characters. Here is writing that is fair and honest without either negative stereotypes on the one hand or pictures of saints on the other.

Notes—Literatura Chicanesca

1. Francisco A. Lomelí and Donaldo W. Urioste, *Chicano Perspectives in Literature: A Critical and Annotated Bibliography* (Albuquerque, NM: Pajarito Publications, 1976) 12.

2. Cecil Robinson, *With the Ears of Strangers: The Mexican in American Literature* (Tucson, AZ: University of Arizona Press, 1963).

3. Cecil Robinson, *Mexico and the Hispanic Southwest in American Literature* (Tucson, AZ: University of Arizona Press, 1977) 349.

4. Antonio Márquez, "Literatura Chicanesca," *A Decade of Chicano Literature 1970–1979*, ed. Luis Leal, Fernando de Necochea, Francisco Lomelí, and Roberto G. Trujillo (Santa Barbara, CA: Editorial La Causa, 1982) 73.

5. Márquez 76.

6. Márquez 79.

7. Edward Simmen, introduction, *The Chicano: From Caricature to Self-Portrait* (New York: New American Library, 1971) 23–24.

LITERATURA CHICANESCA

8. Mary Chavarría, "Amado Jesús Muro," *Chicano Literature: A Reference Guide*, ed. Julio A. Martínez and Francisco A. Lomelí (Westport, CT: Greenwood Press, 1985) 454.

9. John Gregory Dunne, "The Secret of Danny Santiago," *New York Review of Books* 16 Aug. 1984: 25.

10. Rudolfo A. Anaya, introduction, *Los cumpleaños de Doña Agueda*, by Jim Sagel, (Austin, TX: Place of Herons, 1984) i.

11. Márquez 79.

Chicano Literature: A Suggested Reading List

This list is not meant to be comprehensive; it merely provides a reader with a large body of work with which to begin study of Chicano literature. Unless otherwise noted, all quotations from literary works used in *Understanding Chicano Literature* are from the editions cited here; page numbers are included in the text.

Poetry

Alurista. *Floricanto en Aztlán*. Los Angeles: University of California: Chicano Studies Center, 1971.

———. *Nationchild Plumaroja*. San Diego: Toltecas en Aztlán Productions, 1972.

———. *Timespace Huracán: Poems, 1972–1975*. Albuquerque: Pajarito Publications, 1976.

———. *A'nque*. San Diego: Maize Publications, 1979.

———. *Spik in glyph?* Houston: Arte Público Press, 1981.

———. *Return: Poems Collected and New*. Ypsilanti, MI: Bilingual Press/ Editorial Bilingüe, 1982. Contains *Dawn's Eye* and *Nationchild Plumaroja*.

Anaya, Rudolfo. *The Adventures of Juan Chicaspatas*. Houston: Arte Público Press, 1985.

Bruce-Novoa, Juan. *Inocencia perversa/Perverse Innocence*. Phoenix: Baleen Press, 1977.

Candelaria, Cordelia. *Ojo de la Cueva/Cave Springs*. Colorado Springs: Maize Press, 1984.

Cárdenas, Reyes. *Survivors of the Chicano Titanic*. Austin: Place of Herons Press, 1981.

———. *I Was Never a Militant Chicano*. Austin: Relámpago, 1986.

SUGGESTED READING LIST

Castillo, Ana. *Zero Makes Me Hungry.* Greenview, IL: Scott-Foresman, 1975.

———. *I Close My Eyes (To See).* Pullman: Washington State University, 1976.

———. *Women Are Not Roses.* Houston: Arte Público Press, 1984.

Cervantes, Lorna Dee. *Emplumada.* Pittsburgh: University of Pittsburgh Press, 1981.

Chávez, Fray Angélico. *Clothed with the Sun.* Santa Fe: Writer's Editions, 1939.

———. *Eleven Lady-Lyrics and Other Poems.* Paterson, NJ: St. Anthony Guild Press, 1945.

———. *Selected Poems with an Apologia.* Santa Fe: Press of the Territorian, 1969.

Corpi, Lucha. *Palabras de Mediodía/Noon Words.* English translation by Catherine Rodríguez-Nieto. Berkeley: University of California: El Fuego de Aztlán Publications, 1980.

Delgado, Abelardo. *Chicano: 25 Pieces of a Chicano Mind.* Denver: Barrio Publications, 1969.

———. *Bajo el sol de Aztlán: 25 soles de Abelardo.* El Paso: Barrio Publications, 1973.

———. *It's Cold: 52 Cold-Thought Poems of Abelardo.* Salt Lake City: Barrio Publications, 1974.

———. *Reflexiones: 16 Reflections of Abelardo.* Salt Lake City: Barrio Publications, 1976.

———. *Here Lies Lalo: 25 Deaths of Abelardo.* Salt Lake CIty: Barrio Publications, 1977.

———. *Under the Skirt of Lady Justice: 43 Skirts of Abelardo.* Denver: Barrio Publications, 1978.

———. *Unos perros con metralla: 25 perros de Abelardo.* Arvada, CA: Barrio Publications, 1982.

Elizondo, Sergio. *Perros y antiperros: Una Épica Chicana.* English translation by Gustavo Segade. Berkeley, CA: Quinto Sol Publications, 1972.

SUGGESTED READING LIST

———. *Libro para batos y chavalas chicanas*. English translation by Edmundo García Girón. Berkeley, CA: Editorial Justa Publications, 1977.

Gonzales, Rudolfo "Corky." *I Am Joaquín/Yo Soy Joaquín*. New York: Bantam Books, 1972.

Herrera, Juan Felipe. *Exiles of Desire*. Houston: Arte Público Press, 1985.

Hoyos, Angela de. *Chicano Poems for the Barrio*. Bloomington, IN: Backstage Books, 1975.

———. *Arise Chicano! and Other Poems*. Bloomington, IN: Backstage Books, 1975.

———. *Selected Poems/selecciones*. Spanish translation by Mireya Robles. San Antonio: Dezkalzo Press, 1979.

———. *Woman, Woman*. Houston: Arte Público Press, 1985.

Méndez M., Miguel. *Los Criaderos Humanos (Épica de los desamparados) y Sahuaros*. Tucson: Editorial Peregrinos, 1975.

Mora, Pat. *Chants*. Houston: Arte Público Press, 1984.

———. *Borders*. Houston: Arte Público Press, 1986.

Ríos, Alberto. *Elk Heads on the Wall*. Berkeley: University of California, 1979.

———. *Sleeping on Fists*. Story, WY: Dooryard Press, 1981.

———. *Whispering to Fool the Wind*. Riverdale on Hudson, NY: The Sheep Meadow Press, 1984.

———. *Five Indiscretions*. Riverdale on Hudson, NY: The Sheep Meadow Press, 1985.

Rivera, Tomás. *Always and Other Poems*. Sisterdale, TX: Sisterdale Press, 1973.

Romero, Leo. *During the Growing Season*. Tucson: Maguey Press, 1978.

———. *Agua Negra*. Boise: Ahsahta Press, 1981.

———. *Celso*. Houston: Arte Público Press, 1985.

Romero, Lin. *Happy Songs, Bleeding Hearts*. San Diego: Toltecas en Aztlán Publications, 1974.

SUGGESTED READING LIST

Salinas, Luis Omar. *Crazy Gypsy*. Fresno: La Raza Studies, 1970.

——. *I Go Dreaming Serenades*. San Jose, CA: Mango Press, 1979.

——. *Afternoon of the Unreal*. Fresno: Abramas Publications, 1980.

——. *Prelude to Darkness*. San Jose, CA: Mango Press, 1981.

——. *Darkness Under the Trees/Walking Behind the Spanish*. Berkeley: University of California, Chicano Studies Library Publications, 1982.

——. *The Sadness of Days: Selected and New Poems*. Houston: Arte Público Press, 1987.

Salinas, Raúl R. *Un Trip Through the Mind Jail y Otras Excursiones*. San Francisco: Editorial Pocho-Che, 1980.

Sánchez, Ricardo. *Canto y grito mi liberación*. El Paso: Mictla Publications, 1971; rpt. *Canto y grito mi liberación: The Liberation of a Chicano Mind*. Garden City, NY: Anchor Books, 1973.

——. *HechizoSpells*. Los Angeles: University of California, Chicano Studies Center Publications, 1976.

——. *Milhuas Blues y gritos norteños*. Milwaukee: University of Wisconsin, Spanish-Speaking Outreach Institute, 1979.

——. *Brown Bear Honey Madness: Alaskan Cruising Poems*. Edgewood, TX: Slough Press, 1982.

——. *Amsterdam Cantos y poemas pistos*. Austin: Place of Herons, 1983.

——. *Selected Poems*. Houston: Arte Público Press, 1985.

Silva, Beverly. *The Second St. Poems*. Ypsilanti, MI: Bilingual Press/ Editorial Bilingüe, 1983.

Soto, Gary. *The Elements of San Joaquín*. Pittsburgh: University of Pittsburgh Press, 1977.

——. *The Tale of Sunlight*. Pittsburgh: University of Pittsburgh Press, 1978.

SUGGESTED READING LIST

————. *Father Is a Pillow Tied to a Broom*. Pittsburgh: Slow Loris Press, 1980.

————. *Where Sparrows Work Hard*. Pittsburgh: University of Pittsburgh Press, 1981.

————. *Black Hair*. Pittsburgh: University of Pittsburgh Press, 1985.

Tafolla, Carmen. *Curandera*. San Antonio: M&A Editions, 1983.

————. Reyes Cárdenas and Cecilio García-Camarillo. *Get Your Tortillas Together*. San Antonio: Caracol Press, 1976.

Tovar, Inés. *Con razón corazón*. Austin, TX, 1977.

Vigil, Evangelina. *Nada y Nade: A Collection of Poems*. San Antonio: M&A Editions, 1978.

————. *Thirty an' Seen a Lot*. Houston: Arte Público Press, 1982.

————. *The Computer Is Down*. Houston, Arte Público Press, 1987.

Villanueva, Alma. *Bloodroot*. Austin: Place of Herons Press, 1977.

————. *Poems. Third Chicano Literary Prize, Irvine 1976–1977*. Irvine, CA: Department of Spanish and Portuguese, 1977, 85–133.

————. *Mother, May I?* Pittsburgh: Motheroot Publications, 1978.

————. *Lifespan*. Austin: Place of Herons Press, 1984.

Villanueva, Tino. *Hay Otra Voz Poems (1968–1971)*. New York: Editorial Mensaje, 1972.

————. *Shaking Off the Dark*. Houston: Arte Público Press, 1984.

Zamora, Bernice. *Restless Serpents*. Menlo Park, CA: Diseños Literarios, 1976 (bound jointly with José Antonio Burciaga, *Restless Serpents*).

SUGGESTED READING LIST

Theater

Avedaño, Fausto. *El corrido de California*. Berkeley, CA: Editorial Justa Publications, 1979.

Garza, Roberto J., ed. *Contemporary Chicano Theatre*. Notre Dame, IN: University of Notre Dame Press, 1976. Contains eight plays by six authors: *Los vendidos* and *Bernabé* by Luis Valdez; *La raza pura, or Racial, Racial* by Rubén Sierra; *Dawn* by Alurista; *The Ultimate Pendejada* and *Mártir Montezuma* by Ysidro R. Macías; *No Nos Venceremos* by Roberto J. Garza; and *The Day of the Swallows* by Estela Portillo Trambley.

Hernández, Alfonso. *The False Advent of Mary's Child and Other Plays*. Berkeley, CA: Editorial Justa, 1979. Contains the title play; *Every Family Has One*; and *The Imperfect Bachelor*.

Huerta, Jorge A., ed. *El Teatro de la Esperanza: An Anthology of Chicano Drama*. Goleta, CA: El Teatro de la Esperanza, 1973. "Joey's Epitaph" by Joey García; *Trampa sin Salida* by Jaime Verdugo; *Pánfila la Curandera*, a collective work; *Brujerías* by Rodrigo Duarte-Clark; *La Bolsa Negra* by Frank Ramírez; *Los Pelados* by Felipe Castro; "Poema de un Mexicano en Aztlán" by Juan Morales; and *El Renacimiento de Huitzilopochtli* by Jorge A. Huerta. Contains introduction, photos, production notes, and brief biographies of playwrights.

Kanellos, Nicolás and Jorge A. Huerta, eds. *Nuevos Pasos: Chicano and Puerto Rican Drama*. Revista Chicano-Riqueña 7, 1 (1979). Chicano plays are *The Interview* by Ron Arias, *Brujerías* by Rodrigo Duarte-Clark, *Sun Images* by Estela Portillo Trambley, *Rancho Hollywood* by Carlos Morton, and *Manolo* by Rubén Sierra.

León, Nephtalí de. *Five Plays*. Denver: Totinem Publications, 1972. Contains *The Death of Ernesto Nerios*; *Chicanos! The Living and the Dead*; *Play Number 9*; *The Judging of Man*; and *The Flies*.

SUGGESTED READING LIST

Moraga, Cherríe. *Giving Up the Ghost.* Los Angeles: West End Books, 1986.

Morton, Carlos. "El Cuento de Pancho Diablo." *Grito del Sol* 1, 3 (July–Sept. 1976): 39–85.

———. *The Many Deaths of Danny Rosales.* Houston: Arte Público Press, 1983. Includes the title play; *El Jardín; Los Dorados;* and *Rancho Hollywood.*

———. *The Meeting. Hispanics in the United States, Vol. 2,* ed. Franciso A. Jiménez and Gary D. Keller. Ypsilanti, MI: Bilingual Press/Editorial Bilingüe, 1982. 87–99.

Portillo Trambley, Estela. *Sor Juana and Other Plays.* Ypsilanti, MI: Bilingual Press/Editorial Bilingüe, 1983. In addition to the two-act title work contains *Puente Negro; Autumn Gold;* and *Blacklight,* all three-acts.

Valdez, Luis. *Actos.* San Juan Bautista, CA: El Centro Campesino Cultural, 1971. Contains *Las Dos Caras del Patroncito, La Quinta Temporada, Los Vendidos, La Conquista de Mexico, No Saco Nada de la Escuela, The Militants, Huelguistas, Vietnam Campesino,* and *Soldado Razo.*

———. *Dark Root of a Scream. From the Barrio: A Chicano Anthology,* ed. Luis Omar Salinas and Lillian Faderman. San Francisco: Canfield Press, 1973, 79–98.

———. *The Shrunken Head of Pancho Villa. West Coast Plays* 11–12 (Winter and Spring 1982): 1–61.

Novels

Anaya, Rudolfo. *Bless Me, Última.* Berkeley, CA: Quinto Sol Publications, 1972.

———. *Heart of Aztlán.* Berkeley: Editorial Justa Publications, 1976.

———. *Tortuga.* Berkeley, CA: Editorial Justa Publications, 1979.

SUGGESTED READING LIST

————. *The Legend of La Llorona*. Berkeley, CA: Tonatiuh–Quinto Sol International, 1984.

Arias, Ron. *The Road to Tamazunchale*. Reno: West Coast Poetry Review, 1975; rpt. Albuquerque: Pajarito Publications, 1978.

Barrio, Raymund. *The Plum Plum Pickers*. Sunnyvale, CA: Ventura Press, 1969.

Brito, Aristeo. *El diablo en Texas*. Tucson: Editorial Peregrinos, 1976.

Candelaria, Nash. *Memories of the Alhambra*. Palo Alto: Cíbola Press, 1977.

————. *Not by the Sword*. Ypsilanti, MI: Bilingual Press/Editorial Bilingüe, 1982.

————. *Inheritance of Strangers*. Binghamton, NY: Bilingual Press/Editorial Bilingüe, 1985.

Casas, Celso A. de. *Pelón Drops Out*. Berkeley, CA: Tonatiuh International, 1979.

Castillo, Ana. *The Mixquiahuala Letters*. Binghamton, NY: Bilingual Press/Editorial Bilingüe, 1986.

Chacón, Eusebio. *El hijo de la tempestad: Tras la tormenta la calma: Dos novelistas orginales*. Santa Fe: Tipografía de El Boletín Popular, 1892.

Chacón, Felipe Maximiliano. *Obras de Felipe Maximiliano Chacón, El Cantor Neomexicano: Poesía y Prosa*. Albuquerque, 1924.

Delgado, Abelardo. *Letters to Louise*. Berkeley, CA: Tonatiuh–Quinto Sol International, 1982.

Elizondo, Sergio. *Muerte en una estrella*. Mexico City: Tinta Negra Editores, 1984.

García, Lionel G. *Leaving Home*. Houston: Arte Público Press, 1985.

————. *A Shroud in the Family*. Houston: Arte Público Press, 1987.

Hinojosa-Smith, Rolando. *Estampas del valle y otras obras*. En-

SUGGESTED READING LIST

glish translation by Gustavo Valadez. Berkeley, CA: Quinto Sol Publications, 1973. Hinojosa revised and republished this as *The Valley*. Ypsilanti, MI: Bilingual Press/Editorial Bilingüe, 1983.

———. *Klail City y sus alrededores*. Havana, Cuba: Casa de las Américas, 1976. English version, *Generaciones y semblanzas*, translation by Rosaura Sánchez. Berkeley, CA: Editorial Justa Publications, 1977. Author's English version, *Klail City*. Houston: Arte Público Press, 1987.

———. *Korean Love Songs: From Klail City Death Trip*. Berkeley, CA: Editorial Justa Publications, 1978. This is poetry, but is included here because Hinojosa describes it as poetic interlude in the *Klail City Death Trip* novel series.

———. *Mi querido Rafa*. Houston: Arte Público Press, 1981. English version by the author, *Dear Rafe*. Houston: Arte Público Press, 1985.

———. *Rites and Witnesses: A Comedy*. Houston: Arte Público Press, 1982.

———. *Partners in Crime: A Rafe Buenrostro Mystery*. Houston: Arte Público Press, 1985.

———. *Claros varones de Belken/Fair Gentlemen of Belken County*. English translation by Julia Cruz. Tempe, AZ: Bilingual Press/Editorial Bilingüe, 1986.

———. *This Migrant Earth*. Houston: Arte Público Press, 1987. English translation of Tomás Rivera's " . . . y no se lo tragó la tierra."

Islas, Arturo. *The Rain God: A Desert Tale*. Palo Alto, CA: Alexandrian Press, 1984.

Méndez M., Miguel. *Peregrinos de Aztlán*. Tucson: Editorial Peregrinos, 1974.

———. *El sueño de Santa María de las Piedras*. Guadalajara, Mexico: Universidad de Guadalajara, 1986.

SUGGESTED READING LIST

Morales, Alejandro. *Caras viejas y vino nuevo.* Mexico City: Editorial Joaquín Mortiz, 1975. Edited with revised translation by Max Martínez, José Monleón, and Alurista, *Old Faces and New Wine.* San Diego: Maize Press, 1981.

———. *La verdad sin voz.* Mexico City: Editorial Joaquín Mortiz, 1979.

———. *Reto en el paraíso.* Ypsilanti, MI: Bilingual Press/ Editorial Bilingüe, 1983.

Niggli, Josephina. *Mexican Village.* Chapel Hill: University of North Carolina Press, 1945.

Ornelas, Berta. *Come Down from the Mound.* Phoenix: Miter Publishing Company, 1975.

Pineda, Cecile. *Face.* New York: Penguin Books, 1985.

Portillo Trambley, Estela. *Trini.* Binghamton, NY: Bilingual Press/Editorial Bilingüe, 1986.

Rechy, John. *City of Night.* New York: Grove Press, 1963.

———. *This Day's Death.* New York: Grove Press, 1969.

———. *The Fourth Angel.* New York: Viking Press, 1972.

Rico, Armando B. *Three Coffins for Nino Lencho.* Berkeley, CA: Tonatiuh–Quinto Sol International, 1984.

Ríos, Isabella. *Victuum.* Ventura, CA: Diana-Etna, 1976.

Rivera, Tomás. " . . . *y no se lo tragó la tierra"/And the Earth Did Not Part.* English translation by Herminio Ríos. Berkeley, CA: Quinto Sol Publications, 1971.

Romero, Orlando. *Nambé-Year One.* Berkeley, CA: Tonatiuh International, 1976.

Salas, Floyd. *Tattoo the Wicked Cross.* New York: Grove Press, 1967.

———. *What Now My Love.* New York: Grove Press, 1970.

———. *Lay My Body on the Line.* Berkeley, CA: Y'Bird Press, 1978.

Torres-Metzgar, Joseph V. *Below the Summit.* Berkeley, CA:

SUGGESTED READING LIST

Tonatiuh International, 1976.

Valdés, Gina. *There Are No Madmen Here.* San Diego: Maize Press, 1981.

Vásquez, Richard. *Chicano.* Garden City, NY: Doubleday, 1970.

——. *The Giant Killer.* New York: Manor Books, 1978.

——. *Another Land.* New York: Avon Books, 1982.

Venegas, Daniel. *Las aventuras de Don Chipote o Cuando los pericos mamen.* Los Angeles: El Heraldo de México, 1928; rpt. Mexico City: Secretaría de Educación Pública and Centro de Estudios Fronterizos del Norte de México, 1984.

Villarreal, José Antonio. *Pocho.* Garden City, NY: Doubleday, 1959.

——. *The Fifth Horseman.* Garden City, NY: Doubleday, 1974.

——. *Clemente Chacón.* Binghamton, NY: Bilingual Press/ Editorial Bilingüe, 1984.

Villaseñor, Edmund. *Macho!* New York: Bantam Books, 1973.

Short Story Collections

Alarcón, Justo S. *Chulifeas Fronteras.* Albuquerque: Pajarito Publications, 1981.

Anaya, Rudolfo. *The Silence of the Llano.* Berkeley, CA: Tonatiuh–Quinto Sol International, 1982.

Chávez, Fray Angélico. *The Short Stories of Fray Angélico Chávez,* ed. Genaro M. Padilla. Albuquerque: University of New Mexico, 1987.

Chávez, Denise. *The Last of the Menu Girls.* Houston: Arte Público Press, 1986.

Cisneros, Sandra. *The House on Mango Street.* Houston: Arte Público Press, 1983.

Elizondo, Sergio. *Rosa, La Flauta.* Berkeley, CA: Editorial Justa Publications, 1980.

SUGGESTED READING LIST

Griego y Maestas, José and Rudolfo A. Anaya. *Cuentos: Tales from the Hispanic Southwest*. Santa Fe: The Museum of New Mexico Press, 1980. Folktales, adapted in Spanish by Griego y Maestas and retold in English by Anaya.

Keller, Gary (El Huitlacoche). *Tales of El Huitlacoche*. Colorado Springs: Maize Press, 1984.

Martínez, Max. *The Adventures of the Chicano Kid and Other Stories*. Houston: Arte Público Press, 1982.

Méndez M., Miguel. *Cuentos para niños traviesos*. English translations by Eva Price. Berkeley, CA: Editorial Justa Publications, 1979.

———. *Tata Casehua y otros cuentos*. English translations by Eva Price. Berkeley, CA: Editorial Justa Publications, 1980.

Navarro, J. L. *Blue Day on Main Street*. Berkeley, CA: Quinto Sol Publications, 1973.

Portillo Trambley, Estela. *Rain of Scorpions and Other Writings*. Berkeley, CA: Tonatiuh International, 1975.

Ríos, Alberto Alvaro. *The Iguana Killer: Twelve Stories of the Heart*. Lewiston, ID: Blue Moon and Confluence Press, 1984.

Sánchez, Saul. *Hay Plesha Lichans tu di Flac*. Berkeley, CA: Editorial Justa Publications, 1977.

Silva, Beverly. *The Cat and Other Stories*. Tempe, AZ: Bilingual Press/Editorial Bilingüe, 1986.

Soto, Gary. *Living Up the Street: Narrative Recollections*. San Francisco: Strawberry Hill Press, 1985.

———. *Small Faces*. Houston: Arte Público Press, 1986.

Torres, José Acosta. *Cachito Mío*. Berkeley, CA: Quinto Sol Publications, 1973.

Ulibarrí, Sabine Reyes. *Tierra Amarilla: Cuentos de Nuevo Mexico*. Quito, Ecuador: Editorial Casa de la Cultura Ecuatoriana, 1964.

———. *Tierra Amarilla: Stories of New Mexico/Cuentos de Nuevo Mexico*. English translation by Thelma Campbell Nason. Al-

SUGGESTED READING LIST

buquerque: University of New Mexico Press, 1971.

———. *Mi abuela fumaba puros y otros cuentos de Tierra Amarilla/ My Grandma Smoked Cigars and Other Stories of New Mexico.* Berkeley, CA: Quinto Sol Publications, 1977.

———. *Primeros Encuentros/First Encounters.* Ypsilanti, MI: Bilingual Press/Editorial Bilingüe, 1982.

Viramontes, Helena María. *The Moths and Other Stories.* Houston: Arte Público Press, 1985.

Selected Short Stories in Periodicals

Arias, Ron. "The Castle." *The Bilingual Review/La Revista Bilingüe* 3, 2 (May–Aug., 1976): 176–182.

Mena, María Cristina. "Emotions of María Concepción." *Century* 88 (Jan., 1914): 348–59.

———. "Doña Rita's Rivals." *Century* 88 (Sept., 1914): 641–52.

———. "Julian Carrillo." *Century* 89 (Mar., 1915): 753–59.

Suárez, Mario. "El Hoyo." *Arizona Quarterly* 3 (Summer 1947): 112–15.

———. "Señor Garza." *Arizona Quarterly* 3 (Summer 1947): 115–21.

———. "Kid Zopilote." *Arizona Quarterly* 3 (Summer, 1947): 130– 37.

———. "Maestría." *Arizona Quarterly* 4 (Winter 1948): 368–73.

———. "The Migrant." *Revista Chicano-Riqueña* 10, 3 (Fall 1982): 15–30.

Torres, Robert Herman. "Mutiny In Jalisco." *Esquire* Mar. 1935: 37, 167–69.

———. "The Brothers Jiminez." *Esquire* June 1936: 90–91, 138, 140.

Autobiography

Acosta, Oscar Zeta. *The Autobiography of a Brown Buffalo.* San Francisco: Straight Arrow Books, 1972.

SUGGESTED READING LIST

――――. *The Revolt of the Cockroach People.* San Francisco: Straight Arrow Books, 1973.

Galarza, Ernesto. *Barrio Boy.* Notre Dame, IN: University of Notre Dame Press, 1971.

Quinn, Anthony. *The Original Sin: A Self Portrait.* New York: Bantam Books, 1974.

Rodriguez, Richard. *Hunger of Memory: The Education of Richard Rodriguez.* Boston: Godine, 1982.

Literatura Chicanesca

Horgan, Paul. *The Common Heart.* New York: Harper, 1942.

LaFarge, Oliver. *Behind the Mountains.* Boston: Houghton Mifflin, 1956.

Muro, Amado. *The Collected Stories of Amado Muro,* with introduction by William Rintoul. Austin: Thorp Springs Press, 1979.

Nelson, Eugene. *The Bracero.* Berkeley, CA: Thorp Springs Press, 1972.

Nichols, John. *The Milagro Beanfield War.* New York: Holt, Rinehart, 1974.

――――. *The Magic Journey.* New York: Holt, Rinehart, 1978.

――――. *The Nirvana Blues.* New York: Holt, Rinehart, 1981.

Sagel, Jim. *Hablando de brujas y la gente de antes: Poemas del Río Chama.* Austin: Place of Herons Press, 1981.

――――. *Tunomás Honey.* Ypsilanti, MI: Bilingual Press/Editorial Bilingüe, 1983. Spanish and English versions of the same stories.

――――. *Los cumpleaños de Doña Agueda.* Austin: Place of Herons Press, 1984. Poetry in both Spanish and English.

Santiago, Danny. *Famous All Over Town.* New York: Simon and Schuster, 1983.

Waters, Frank. *People of the Valley.* New York: Farrar & Rinehart, 1941.

.

Anthologies or Collections

Aguilar, Ricardo, Armando Armengol and Oscar U. Somoza, eds. *Palabra nueva: Cuentos Chicanos.* El Paso: Texas Western Press, 1984. Fifteen stories, all in Spanish.

Anaya, Rudolfo A., ed. *Voces: An Anthology of Nuevo Mexicano Writers.* Albuquerque: El Norte Publications, 1987. Contemporary poetry and prose in Spanish and in English by many residents and natives of New Mexico.

————. Antonio Márquez, eds. *Cuentos Chicanos: A Short Story Anthology.* Albuquerque: University of New Mexico Press, 1984. Twenty-one stories, most of them in English, by many established writers.

Arellano, Anselmo, ed. *Los pobladores nuevomexicanos y su poesía, 1889–1950.* Albuquerque: Pajarito Publications, 1976. Poetry compiled from magazines and newspapers. Provides historical perspective to modern Chicano poetry.

Binder, Wolfgang, ed. *Contemporary Chicano Poetry: An Anthology.* Erlangen, Germany: Verlag Palm & Enke Erlangen, 1986. A European collection, a manifestation of the importance of Chicano poetry abroad.

Boza, María del Carmen, Beverly Silva, and Carmen Valle, eds. *Nosotras: Latina Literature Today.* Binghamton, NY: Bilingual Review/Press, 1986. Thirty-five selections by authors from major Latin communities of the United States.

Cárdenas de Dwyer, Carlota, ed. *Chicano Voices.* Boston: Houghton Mifflin, 1975. A superb introduction for the Anglo student. Accompanied by a highly useful Instructor's Guide.

Daydi-Tolson, Santiago, ed. *Five Poets of Aztlán.* Binghamton, NY: Bilingual Press/Editorial Bilingüe, 1985. Contains an introductory essay by the editor and poetry by Alfonso Rodríguez, El Huitlacoche, Leroy V. Quintana, Alma Villanueva, and Carmen Tafolla.

SUGGESTED READING LIST

Delgado, Abelardo, Ricardo Sánchez, Raymundo Pérez, Juan Valdez. *Los Cuatro.* Denver: Barrio Publications, 1970. One of the earliest poetry anthologies; contains the work of the authors.

Harth, Dorothy E. and Lewis M. Baldwin, eds. *Voices of Aztlán: Chicano Literature Today.* New York: New American Library, 1974. Prose, poetry, and theater.

Hernández, Guillermo, ed. *Canciones de la Raza/Songs of the Chicano Experience.* Berkeley, CA: El Fuego de Aztlan, 1978. Music, lyrics, illustrations, and translations of twelve popular Chicano folk ballads of the twentieth century.

Jiménez, Francisco and Gary D. Keller, eds. *Hispanics in the United States: An Anthology of Creative Literature, Vol. 2.* Ypsilanti, MI: Bilingual Review/Press, 1982. Prose, poetry, and theater.

Kanellos, Nicolás, ed. *A Decade of Hispanic Literature: An Anniversary Anthology.* Special issue of *Revista Chicano-Riqueña* 10, 1–2 (Winter–Spring, 1982). Poetry, prose, and essays by forty-four authors.

———— and Luis Dávila, eds. *Latino Short Fiction.* Special issue of *Revista Chicano-Riqueña* 8, 1 (Winter, 1980). Prize-winning works by Chicanos, Puerto Ricans, Colombians, Peruvians, Cubans, and Chileans living in the United States.

————. *Los Tejanos: A Texas Mexican Anthology.* Special issue of *Revista Chicano-Riqueña* 8, 3 (Verano, 1980). Poetry, prose, an essay, an interview, critical studies, reviews, and artwork.

Keller, Gary D. and Francisco Jiménez, eds. *Hispanics in the United States: An Anthology of Creative Literature.* Ypsilanti, MI: Bilingual Review/Press, 1980. Prose, poetry, and theater.

Ludwig, Ed and James Santibañez, eds. *The Chicanos: Mexican American Voices.* Baltimore: Penguin Books, 1971. Essays, short stories, and selections from novels.

SUGGESTED READING LIST

Ortego, Philip D., ed. *We Are Chicanos: An Anthology of Mexican-American Literature.* New York: Pocket Books, 1973. Background history, folklore, poetry, drama, fiction.

Paley, Julian, ed. *Best New Chicano Literature 1986.* Binghamton, NY: Bilingual Press/Editorial Bilingüe, 1986. Award-winning stories and poems from the Ninth Chicano Literary Contest held at the University of California, Irvine.

Paredes, Américo and Raymund Paredes, eds. *Mexican-American Authors.* Boston: Houghton Mifflin, 1972. Early collection of prose and poetry, designed as a textbook for beginning students.

Romano V., Octavio I. and Herminio Ríos-C., eds. *El Espejo/The Mirror.* Berkeley, CA: Quinto Sol Publications, 1969. The first anthology of Chicano literature; the introduction states that it is compiled and written by "Chicanos without any single obligation to be largely and submissively grateful to Anglo-American foundations and editors."

Salinas, Luis Omar and Lillian Faderman, eds. *From the Barrios: A Chicano Anthology.* New York: Canfield Press, 1973. Essays, poems, plays, fiction. Two parts reflecting the themes "My Revolution" and "My House."

Simmen, Edward, ed. *The Chicanos: From Caricature to Self-Portrait.* New York: New American Library, 1971. Short fiction by Mexican-Americans, plus stories by Anglo writers who depict Chicanos in their work.

Shular, Antonio Castañeda, Tomás Ybarra-Frausto, and Joseph Sommers, eds. *Literatura Chicana: Texto y Contexto/Chicano Literature: Text and Context.* Englewood Cliffs, NJ: Prentice-Hall, 1972. A bilingual collection that presents Chicano, Mexican, Puerto Rican, and some other Latin American literature.

Valdez, Luis and Stan Steiner, eds. *Aztlán: An Anthology of Mexican American Literature.* New York: Vintage Books, 1972.

SUGGESTED READING LIST

Selections from Pre-Columbian Mexico to the late 1960s, divided thematically.

Vigil, Evangelina, ed. *Woman of Her Word: Hispanic Women Write*. Houston: Arte Público Press, 1983. Special issue of *Revista Chicano-Riqueña* 11, 3–4 (Fall–Winter, 1983). Prose, poetry, and art by Chicana, Puerto Rican, Cuban, and other Latin American women.

Villanueva, Tino, comp. *Chicanos: Antología Histórica y Literaria*. Mexico City: Fondo de Cultura Económica, 1980. Spanish-language collection of essays, poetry, prose, and theater.

Language

Bowen, J. Donald and Jacob Ornstein, eds. *Studies in Southwest Spanish*. Rowley, MA: Newbury House, 1976. Nine linguistic essays.

Galván, Roberto A. and Richard V. Teschner. *El Diccionario del Español Chicano/The Dictionary of Chicano Spanish*. Lincolnwood, IL: National Textbook Company, 1985. A Spanish-to-English compilation of over 8,000 words and expressions used by Chicanos. It does not include standard Spanish, only language peculiar to the Chicano.

Hernández-Chávez, Eduardo, Andrew D. Cohen and Anthony F. Beltramo, eds. *El Lenguaje de los Chicanos Regional and Social Characteristics Used by Mexican-Americans*. Arlington, VA: Center for Applied Linguistics, 1975. Twenty essays (two in Spanish), including one on code-switching.

Ornstein-Galícia, Jacob L., ed. *Form and Function in Chicano English*. Rowley, MA: Newbury House, 1984. Essays, one of which treats novels: *Pocho; Bless Me, Última*; and *The Road to Tamazunchale*.

Penfield, Joyce and Jacob L. Ornstein-Galícia. *Chicano English:*

SUGGESTED READING LIST

An Ethnic Contact Dialect. Amsterdam and Philadelphia: John Benjamins Publishing Company, 1985. A linguistic study with a chapter on Chicano speech in written and electronic media.

History and General Background
Books

Acuña, Rodolfo. *Occupied America: The Chicano's Struggle Toward Liberation*. San Francisco: Canfield Press, 1972. U.S. history from a Chicano perspective.

Alford, Harold J. *The Proud Peoples: The Heritage and Culture of Spanish-Speaking Peoples in the United States*. New York: McKay, 1972. Represents all Hispanic groups in the country and includes brief biographies of sixty people, both prominent figures and ordinary folks.

Brenner, Anita. *The Wind That Swept Mexico: The History of the Mexican Revolution 1910–1942*. New York: Harper, 1943. A classic work; 100 pages of text and 184 news photographs documenting the war.

Chávez, John R. *The Lost Land: The Chicano Image of the Southwest*. Albuquerque: University of New Mexico Press, 1984. A view of the history of the Southwest from a Chicano perspective; employs the idea of Aztlán as a central motif.

Durán, Livie Isauro and H. Russel Bernard, eds. *Introduction to Chicano Studies*. 2d ed. New York: Macmillan, 1982. History, migration and labor, education, and culture of the Chicano.

Galarza, Ernesto. *Merchants of Labor: The Mexican Bracero Story*. Santa Barbara, CA: McNally & Loftin, 1964. A classic study of Mexican migratory workers.

García, Richard A. *The Chicanos in America 1540–1974*. Dobbs Ferry, NY: Oceana Publications, 1977. A reference work containing historical documents and bibliographies of art, history, literature, etc.

Garreau, Joel. *The Nine Nations of North America*. Boston: Houghton Mifflin, 1981. The chapter "Mexamerica" is a survey of the U.S.-Mexican border region.

McWilliams, Carey. *North from Mexico: The Spanish-Speaking People of the United States*. Philadelphia: Lippincott, 1949; rpt. New York: Greenwood Press, 1968. A much-respected, classic treatment of Chicano history and heritage.

Meier, Matt S. and Feliciano Rivera. *The Chicanos: A History of Mexican Americans*. New York: Hill and Wang, 1972. A seminal study; focus is on the last two hundred years.

Mirandé, Alfredo and Evangelina Enríquez. *La Chicana*. Chicago: University of Chicago Press, 1979. Studies the role of women in Chicano society; contains a long chapter on "Images in Literature."

Moore, Joan W. with Alfredo Cuellar. *Mexican Americans*. Englewood Cliffs, NJ: Prentice-Hall, 1970. A short but useful introduction to history, education, self-image, language, politics, religion. Good graphs, charts, and tables.

Moquin, Wayne with Charles Van Doren. *A Documentary History of the Mexican Americans*. New York: Praeger, 1971. Sixty-five historical documents with commentary.

Nelson, Eugene. *Pablo Cruz and the American Dream*. Layton, UT: Peregrine Smith Books, 1975. The experiences of an undocumented Mexican working in the United States; a transcription.

Paz, Octavio. *The Labyrinth of Solitude: Life and Thought in Mexico*. Translated by Lysander Kemp. New York: Grove Press, 1961. Highly regarded work on Mexican psychology, originally published in 1950. First chapter, "The *Pachuco* and Other Extremes," is significant for Chicano studies.

Rosenbaum, Robert J. *Mexicano Resistance in the Southwest*.

SUGGESTED READING LIST

Austin: University of Texas Press, 1981. History of cultural conflicts in the second half of the 1800s in New Mexico, Texas, and California.

Steiner, Stan. *La Raza: The Mexican Americans.* New York: Harper, 1969. A discussion of both history and literature, including excerpts from poetry and drama.

Articles

Anaya, Rudolfo. "At the Crossroads." *New Mexico Magazine* 65, 6 (June 1987): 61–64. A writer's look back at the old ways of Hispanic New Mexicans and his reflections on the changes they are undergoing.

Morgan, Thomas B. "The Latinization of America." *Esquire* May, 1983: 47–56. Discusses all Spanish-speaking groups; reflects on their future impact in the United States.

Rodriguez, Richard. "Mexico's Children." *The American Scholar* Spring, 1986: 161–77. A personal account of growing up as a Chicano. Covers language, education, politics, and assimilation.

Womack, John, Jr. "The Chicanos." *New York Review of Books* 31 Aug. 1972: 12–18. Historical survey; short bibliography.

BIBLIOGRAPHY

General Literature
Bibliographies

Eger, Ernestina. *A Bibliography of Criticism of Chicano Literature.* Berkeley, CA: Chicano Studies Library, 1982. A milestone collection; contains published and unpublished work as well as papers presented at conferences.

Heisley, Michael, comp. *An Annotated Bibliography of Chicano Folklore from the Southwestern United States.* Los Angeles: University of California, 1977. Over one thousand entries; a project funded by the U.S. Government, Ethnic Heritage Studies Program.

Lomelí, Francisco A. and Donaldo W. Urioste. *Chicano Perspectives in Literature: A Critical and Annotated Bibliography.* Albuquerque: Pajarito Publications, 1976. Much-cited, highly regarded early bibliography; contains the origin of the term *literatura chicanesca.*

Ordóñez, Elizabeth J. "Chicana Literature and Related Sources: A Selected and Annotated Bibliography." *The Bilingual Review/La Revista Bilingüe* 7, 2 (May–Aug. 1980) 143–64. Covers, in the 198 entries, literature, folklore, history, criticism, film, and other activities by the women in Chicano society.

Romano V., Octavio I., ed. *Toward a Chicano/Raza Bibliography.* *El Grito* 7, 2 (Dec. 1973): 1–85. Extensive unannotated listing of drama, prose, and poetry; appendix has a serial listing.

Trujillo, Robert G. and Andrés Rodríguez. *Literatura Chicana: Creative and Critical Writings Through 1984.* Oakland, CA: Floricanto Press, 1985. Comprehensive listing of 783 works; includes literature and non-literary materials.

Zimmerman, Enid. "An Annotated Bibliography of Chicano

BIBLIOGRAPHY

Literature: Novels, Short Fiction, Poetry and Drama, 1970–1980." *The Bilingual Review/La Revista Bilingüe* 9, 3 (Sept.–Dec. 1982): 227–50. Contains an introduction, 162 entries, and brief description of nine journals.

Books

Baker, Houston A., Jr. *Three American Literatures: Essays in Chicano, Native American, and Asian-American Literature for Teachers of American Literature.* New York: the Modern Language Association of America, 1982. Contains "Chicano Literature," by Luis Leal and Pepe Barrón, and "The Evolution of Chicano Literature," by Raymund A. Paredes, a revised and expanded version of the *MELUS* article cited below

Bruce-Novoa. *Chicano Authors: Inquiry by Interview.* Austin: University of Texas Press, 1980. Much biographical information on fourteen major Chicano writers.

Fisher, Dexter, ed. *Minority Language and Literature: Retrospective and Perspective.* New York: Modern Language Association, 1977. Papers presented at a national symposium on minority literature, New York City, November, 1976.

García, Eugene E., Francisco A. Lomelí and Isidro D. Ortiz, eds. *Chicano Studies: A Multidisciplinary Approach.* New York: Teachers College Press, 1984. Essays on history, politics, literature, folklore, and education.

Herrera-Sobek, María, ed. *Beyond Stereotypes: The Critical Analysis of Chicana Literature.* Binghamton, NY: Bilingual Press/Editorial Bilingüe, 1985. Six articles (four on prose, two on poetry) treating women in Chicano literature as well as women writers.

Jiménez, Francisco, ed. *The Identification and Analysis of Chicano Literature.* Binghamton, NY: Bilingual Press/Editorial Bilingüe, 1979. Treats the problem of identifying and distinguishing Chicano literature from Mexican and American; themes, myths, folklore, language.

BIBLIOGRAPHY

Leal, Luis. *Aztlán y México: Perfiles literarios e históricos.* Binghamton, NY: Bilingual Press/Editorial Bilingüe, 1985. Essays relating Chicano and Mexican literature and culture.
———. Fernando de Necochea, Francisco Lomelí and Roberto G. Trujillo, eds. *A Decade of Chicano Literature, 1970–1979: Critical Essays and Bibliography.* Santa Barbara, CA: Editorial La Causa, 1982. Covers all genres; papers from a 1980 conference at the University of California, Santa Barbara.

Martínez, Julio A. and Francisco A. Lomelí. *Chicano Literature: A Reference Guide.* Westport, CT: Greenwood Press, 1985. Indispensable reference work for any student of Chicano literature; contains hundreds of entries, excellent bibliographies, a glossary, and a useful chronology.

Sommers, Joseph and Tomás Ybarra-Frausto, eds. *Modern Chicano Writers.* Englewood Cliffs, NJ: Prentice-Hall, 1979. Excellent collection of critical essays.

Tatum, Charles M. *Chicano Literature.* Boston: Twayne, 1982. A comprehensive study; includes much information about literature prior to 1960 and a great deal on modern works through 1980.

Articles

Bruce-Novoa. "Canonical and Noncanonical Texts." *The Americas Review* 14, 3–4 (Fall-Winter 1986) 119–35. A brief history of the Chicano novel, focusing on how works and writers are included or excluded from the literary canon.

Paredes, Raymund A. "The Evolution of Chicano Literature." *MELUS* 5, 2 (Summer 1978): 71–110. An insightful survey, published by the Society for the Study of Multi-Ethnic Literature of the United States.
———. "Mexican American Authors and the American Dream." *MELUS* 8, 4 (Winter 1981): 71–80. Traces the theme of the American dream through poetry, short story, autobiography, and novel.

BIBLIOGRAPHY

Poetry
Books

Binder, Wolfgang, ed. *Partial Autobiographies: Interviews with Twenty Chicano Poets.* Erlangen, Germany: Verlag Palm & Enke Erlangen, 1985. A significant collection by one of Europe's leading scholars.

Bruce-Novoa. *Chicano Poetry: A Response to Chaos.* Austin: University of Texas Press, 1982. Scholarly treatment of the writings of the major contemporary poets.

Candelaria, Cordelia. *Chicano Poetry: A Critical Introduction.* Westport CT: Greenwood Press, 1986. Covers writers working since 1967; focuses on high quality and those who have received the most critical attention.

Paredes, Américo. *"With His Pistol in His Hand": A Border Ballad and Its Hero.* Austin: University of Texas Press, 1958. A study of one of the most famous *corridos*; also interpretations of the border country, its history and people.

Sánchez, Marta Ester. *Contemporary Chicana Poetry: A Critical Approach to an Emerging Literature.* Berkeley: University of California Press, 1985. Treats poetry written by women: Alma Villanueva, Lorna Dee Cervantes, Lucha Corpi, and Bernice Zamora.

Articles

Bornstein-Somoza, Miriam. "The Voice of the Chicana in Poetry." *Denver Quarterly* 16, 3 (Fall 1981): 28–47. Focus on women poets.

Bruce-Novoa. "Chicano Poetry." *Chicano Literature: A Reference Guide,* ed. Julio A. Martínez and Francisco A. Lomelí. Westport, CT: Greenwood Press, 1985. 161–73. A survey, with emphasis on post-1965 period; large number of authors treated.

———. "The Other Voice of Silence: Tino Villanueva." *Modern*

BIBLIOGRAPHY

Chicano Writers, ed. Joseph Sommers and Tomás Ybarra-Frausto. Englewood Cliffs, NJ: Prentice-Hall, 1979. 133–140. Discusses writings of one of the most outstanding contemporary Chicano poets.

Cárdenas de Dwyer, Carlota. "Poetry." *A Decade of Chicano Literature, 1970–1979: Critical Essays and Bibliography*, ed. Luis Leal et al. Santa Barbara, CA: Editorial La Causa, 1982. 19–28. Treats poetry of the 1970s; discusses major authors and works and the changing social climate which fosters Chicano poetry.

Hancock, Joel. "The Emergence of Chicano Poetry: A Survey of Sources, Themes and Techniques," *Arizona Quarterly* 29 (Spring 1973): 57–73. A good article for a student to use as a starting point for study of Chicano poetry.

Herrera-Sobek, María. "The Acculturation Process of the Chicana in the Corrido." *Proceedings of the Pacific Coast Council on Latin American Studies* 9 (1982): 25–34. Discusses the folk ballad and its depiction of women; examines new perspectives brought about by acculturation.

Meyer, Doris L. "Anonymous Poetry in Spanish-Language New Mexico Newspapers, 1880–1900." *Bilingual Review/Revista Bilingüe* 2, 3 (Sept.–Dec. 1975): 259–75. Significant study which establishes a poetic tradition among nineteenth-century Mexican-Americans.

Ortega y Gasca, Felipe de. "An Introduction to Chicano Poetry." *Modern Chicano Writers*, ed. Joseph Sommers and Tomás Ybarra-Frausto. Englewood Cliffs, NJ: Prentice-Hall, 1979. 108–16.

Seator, Lynette. "*Emplumada*: Chicana Rites of Passage." *MELUS* 11, 2 (Summer 1984): 23–38. Discussion of a collection by Lorna Dee Cervantes; approaches it as a unified whole with the theme of coming of age.

BIBLIOGRAPHY

Soto, Gary. "Luis Omar Salinas: Chicano Poet." *MELUS* 9, 2 (Summer 1982): 47–82. An examination of the poet's life and work up to 1970.

Ybarra-Frausto, Tomás. "The Chicano Movement and the Emergence of a Chicano Poetic Consciousness." *New Scholar* 6, (1977): 81–109. Survey of early poets of the 1960s and 1970s; discusses many poets who published in newspapers and periodicals.

Theater
Books

Chicano Theatre One. San Juan Bautista, CA: La Cucaracha Press, 1973. Contains essays on Chicano theater, poetry, reviews, and a play, "La trampa sin salida," by Jaime Verdugo.

Huerta, Jorge A. *Chicano Theater: Themes and Forms.* Ypsilanti, MI: Bilingual Press/Editorial Bilingüe, 1982. The definitive critical survey to date.

Kanellos, Nicolás. *Two Centuries of Hispanic Theatre in the Southwest.* Houston: Revista Chicano-Riqueña, 1982. A useful monograph for background history of theater.

———. *Mexican American Theater: Legacy and Reality.* Pittsburgh: Latin American Literary Review Press, 1987. Seven essays by this author, six selected from articles previously published in journals.

———. *Mexican American Theatre: Then and Now.* Houston: Arte Público Press, 1983. Special issue of *Revista Chicano-Riqueña* 11, 1 (Spring 1983). Contains plays, critical studies, and interviews.

Jones, Willis Knapp. *Behind Spanish American Footlights.* Austin: University of Texas Press, 1966. Chapter 1, "Pre-Columbian Drama in America," and chapter 31, "Mexico's

217

BIBLIOGRAPHY

Theatre over 375 Years," provide historical information pertinent to the study of Chicano theater.

El Teatro Campesino: The First Twenty Years. San Juan Bautista, CA: El Teatro Campesino, 1985. A compilation of articles, notes, and photographs; depicts the evolution of America's first Chicano theater company, 1965–1985.

Valdez, Luis. *Actos: El Teatro Campesino.* San Juan Bautista, CA: La Cucaracha Press, 1971. Introductory information, "Notes on Chicano Theatre," and "Actos" are important for an understanding of the early work of El Teatro Campesino.

Articles

Brokaw, John W. "A Mexican-American Acting Company, 1849–1924." *Educational Theatre Journal* 17 (Mar. 1975): 23–29. Illustrates the Spanish-speaking dramatic tradition in the United States by examining the history of one theater troupe.

Englekirk, John E. "Notes on the Repertoire of the New Mexican Spanish Folk Theatre." *Southern Folklore Quarterly* 4 (1940): 227–37. A historical study with copies of manuscripts of New Mexico folk plays.

Espinosa, Aureliano M. and J. Manuel Espinosa. "The Texans." *New Mexico Quarterly Review* 13 (1943): 299–308. A translation of this early play.

Huerta, Jorge A. "Chicano Agit-Prop: The Early *Actos* of El Teatro Campesino." *Latin American Theatre Review* 10, 2 (Spring 1977): 45–57. Good analyses of the most popular early pieces.

Jiménez, Francisco. "Dramatic Principles of the Teatro Campesino." *The Bilingual Review/La Revista Bilingüe*, 2, 1–2 (Jan.-Aug. 1975): 99–111. Objectives, content, form, style, technique, language, actors, audience, funding, and influence of El Teatro Campesino.

BIBLIOGRAPHY

Kanellos, Nicolás. "Mexican Community Theatre in a Midwestern City." *Latin American Theatre Review* 7, 1 (Fall 1973): 43–47. An introduction to Mexican-American theater in East Chicago, Indiana, in the 1920s.

———. "The Flourishing of Hispanic Theatre in the Southwest, 1920–30's." *Latin American Theatre Review* 16, 1 (Fall 1982): 29–40. A slightly different, more fully annotated version of the monograph cited above.

Leinaweaver, Richard E. "*Rabinal Achí*: Commentary" and "*Rabinal Achí*: English Translation." *Latin American Theatre Review* 1, 2 (Spring 1968): 3–54. Discussion and translation of the best example of indigenous drama of North and South America.

Matson, Eva Jane. "Los Pastores del Valle de Mesilla: Packing Them in for 25 Years." *New Mexico Magazine* Dec. 1985: 59–62. Account of contemporary productions of drama from the sixteenth century.

Parker, Robert A. "The Pachuco World of Luis Valdez." *Americas* Aug. 1979: 3–8. Discussion of Broadway production of *Zoot Suit* and interview with Valdez.

Pross, Edith E. "A Chicano Play and Its Audience." *The Americas Review* 14, 1 (Spring 1986): 71–79. Treats audience reaction to *The Many Deaths of Danny Rosales*, by Carlos Morton.

Ybarra-Frausto, Tomás. "Punto de Partida." *Latin American Theatre Review* 4, 2 (Spring 1971): 51–52. Short but informative survey of pre-1965 Chicano drama.

Novel and Short Story
Books

Lattin, Vernon E., ed. *Contemporary Chicano Fiction: A Critical Survey.* Binghamton, NY: Bilingual Press/Editorial Bilingüe, 1986. Twenty-six articles and a bibliography.

Lewis, Marvin A. *Introduction to the Chicano Novel.* Milwaukee:

BIBLIOGRAPHY

University of Wisconsin Spanish-Speaking Outreach Institute, 1982. A monograph taking a culturalist approach to works by leading novelists.

Olivares, Julián, ed. *International Studies in Honor of Tomás Rivera*. Houston: Arte Público Press, 1986. A special double edition of the *Revista Chicano-Riqueña* 13, 3–4 (Fall-Winter 1985) with essays on Rivera's work, other Chicano literature, and dedicatory commentary.

Rodríguez del Pino, Salvador. *La Novela Chicana Escrita en Español: Cinco Autores Comprometidos* (The Chicano Novel Written in Spanish: Five Committed Authors). Ypsilanti, MI: Bilingual Press/Editorial Bilingüe, 1982. Contains chapters on Tomás Rivera, Miguel Méndez, Alejandro Morales, Aristeo Brito, and Rolando Hinojosa.

Saldívar, José David. *The Rolando Hinojosa Reader: Essays Historical and Critical*. Houston: Arte Público Press, 1985. Special edition of *Revista Chicano-Riqueña* 12, 3–4 (Fall-Winter 1984). Essays by and about Hinojosa and his work, including an interview.

Vassallo, Paul, ed. *The Magic of Words: Rudolfo A. Anaya and His Writings*. Albuquerque: University of New Mexico Press, 1982. Essays by and about Anaya; includes an annotated bibliography.

Articles

Cárdenas de Dwyer, Carlota. "International Literary Metaphor and Ron Arias: An Analysis of *The Road to Tamazunchale*." *The Identification and Analysis of Chicano Literature*, ed. Francisco Jiménez. Binghamton, NY: Bilingual Press/Editorial Bilingüe, 1979. 358–64.

Márquez, Antonio. "The American Dream in the Chicano Novel." *Rocky Mountain Review* 39 (1983): 4–19. Investigation of the Chicano facet of an important theme in American literature.

BIBLIOGRAPHY

Saldívar, Ramón. "A Dialectic of Difference: Towards a Theory of the Chicano Novel." *MELUS* 6, 3 (Fall 1979): 73–92. Discussion of several novels with the intent of establishing critical approaches.

Tatum, Charles. "Some Examples of Chicano Prose Fiction of the Nineteenth and Early Twentieth Centuries." *Revista Chicano-Riqueña* 9, 4 (Winter 1981): 58–67. Discusses works by Benjamín Padilla, Julio G. Arce, Eusebio Falcón, María Esperanza Pardo, Laura de Pereda, and others.

Vallejos, Tomás. "Ritual Process and the Family in the Chicano Novel." *MELUS* 10, 4 (Winter 1983): 5–16. Treatment of *Pocho, Bless Me, Última,* and " . . . *y no se lo tragó la tierra.*"

Autobiography

Alurista. "Acosta's *The Revolt of the Cockroach People:* The Case, The Novel, and History." *Contemporary Chicano Fiction: A Critical Survey,* ed. Vernon E. Lattin. Binghamton, NY: Bilingual Press/Editorial Bilingüe, 1986. 94–104.

Márquez, Antonio. "Richard Rodriguez's *Hunger of Memory* and the Poetics of Experience." *Arizona Quarterly* 40 (Summer 1984): 130–41. Provides a basis for critical analysis of a controversial book.

Rivera, Tomás. "Richard Rodriguez' *Hunger of Memory* as Humanistic Antithesis." *MELUS* 11, 4 (Winter 1985): 5–13. An essay explaining and refuting the ideas expounded in the autobiography.

Smith, Norman D. "Buffalos and Cockroaches: Acosta's Siege at Aztlan." *Contemporary Chicano Fiction: A Critical Survey,* ed. Vernon E. Lattin. Binghamton, NY: Bilingual Press/ Editorial Bilingüe, 1986. 82–93.

Literatura Chicanesca
Books

Pettit, Arthur G. *Images of the Mexican American in Fiction and*

BIBLIOGRAPHY

Film. College Station: Texas A&M University Press, 1980. Surveys the Anglo-American attitude toward the Mexican people of the Southwest as reflected in stereotypes in popular literature and film.

Robinson, Cecil. *With the Ears of Strangers: The Mexican in American Literature.* Tucson: University of Arizona Press, 1963. A classic work; discusses the influence of Mexico on U.S. literature.

———. *Mexico and the Hispanic Southwest in American Literature* Tucson: University of Arizona Press, 1977. A revised edition of *With the Ears of Strangers*, with the addition of a chapter on Chicano literature.

Wild, Peter. *John Nichols.* Boise: Boise State University, 1986. A monograph surveying all of the writer's novels and discussing the criticism of them.

Articles

Dunne, John Gregory. "The Secret of Danny Santiago." *New York Review of Books* 16 Aug. 1984: 17–27. Reveals that Danny Santiago is a pseudonym and discusses Daniel James's reasons for disguising his real identity.

Haslam, Gerald. "The Enigma of Amado Jesús Muro." *Western American Literature* 10, 1 (May 1975): 3–9.

———. "A Question of Authenticity or Who Can Write What." *Western American Literature* 20, 3 (Fall 1985): 246–50.

McMurtry, Larry. "The Pale Chicano." *New York Times Book Review* 30 May 1982. A review of *The Collected Stories of Amado Muro* with notes on Chester Seltzer's life.

Márquez, Antonio. "A Discordant Image: The Mexican in American Literature." *Minority Voices* 5 (Spring 1983): 41–51. Assesses, through literary analysis, cultural differences and conflicts that impede understanding between the United States and Mexico.

Ortego y Gasca, Felipe de. "Danny Santiago and the Ethics of

BIBLIOGRAPHY

Deception." *Nuestro* Nov. 1984: 50–51. A review article; discussion of literary authenticity and deception.

Robinson, Cecil. "The Extended Presence: Mexico and Its Culture in North American Writing." *MELUS* 5, 3 (Fall 1978): 3–15. Survey of images, from earliest times through Katharine Anne Porter and John Nichols.

INDEX

This index does not include material in the Notes, Suggested Reading List, and Bibliography.

INDEX

INDEX

INDEX